Raising Spiritual Children is a beautifully written book that fills a massive gap. I don't know of anyone else who has done what Patty Mapes has achieved here in providing a genuinely charismatic approach to parenting. This is a rare gift to the Body of Christ in general and to Christian families in particular. No parent can afford to be without this practical and prophetic resource. It will empower parents to draw out and cultivate the spiritual gifts that the Perfect Parent, Abba Father, has given to every Christian child. I wish I had read something like this twenty years ago, before the birth of the first of our four children!

Dr. Mark Stibbe
Leader and founder, Father's House Trust
www.fathershousetrust.com

I want to encourage you not just to read but study Patty's book, *Raising Spiritual Children*. Within its pages you will discover much-needed tools to help you with the most important task on Earth: training up the next generation.

Bobby Conner
Founder and president, EaglesView Ministries
www.bobbyconner.org

Raising Spiritual Children not only brings out all the important components of spiritual and prophetic living, but they are presented in a way that will help you tangibly apply them to your family today. Although this book was written for parents, I think it has a broader application for grandparents, teachers, and mentors as well. I have known Greg and Patty and their family for over twenty years, including a number of years when Greg was on my staff. They are excellent people who seek to fully walk out in their personal life and family what they teach. In addition to all of their leadership and experiences, the lives of their children are testimony enough to recommend this book.

Mike Bickle
International House of Prayer of Kansas City

Patricia and Greg Mapes have an important message for parents today with their singular focus on how to develop and protect our spiritually attuned children as they grow. They build on a firm foundation of character development first, and then give us specifics we need to guide us through the common pitfalls usually seen as we try to raise spiritually gifted children.

They draw from their extensive ministry experience as well as their parenting experiences while raising four children, all now grown. They truly give us a fresh and challenging look at this formidable task.

As a licensed clinical psychologist for thirty-seven years, I find their work especially informative and a fun read. Much of the content addresses issues that have been traditionally in the psychological arena, but they add the supernatural to it, bringing together insights on handling the realm of dreams as well as nightmares and night terrors. It is a must-read for parents who know they have spiritually gifted children and have given up searching for any help in this arena.

Dr. Michael A. Campion, PhD, LP, HSPP, CPQ
President, Campion, Barrow and Associates, Inc.

You'll never doubt your influence as a parent after reading Patty Mapes' book, *Raising Spiritual Children*! Every mom and dad who wants to have spiritual influence over this generation needs to grasp these principles. You can shape the character and destiny of others through the principles Patty shares in this groundbreaking book. Read it and be encouraged as you help shape the lives of those you love!

Brian Simmons
Stairway Ministries
www.stairwayministries.org

Proverbs 22:6 instructs us to train up a child in the way he should go, and then when he is old, he will not depart from it. What exactly does that actually mean from a biblical standpoint? For some parents, it simply means trying to impart knowledge of right versus wrong. God, however, as the ultimate Father, is much more thorough and complete in how He wonderfully creates each of us to walk through life in a unique way with unique gifting.

Few parenting books really delve into truly understanding the art of training children to know the Person of God, His ways, and the particulars of His gifting and calling on their lives. Patty and Greg are to be greatly commended for writing *Raising Spiritual Children*, especially as it has not come out of mere theory but authenticity and fruitful experience. I believe *Raising Spiritual Children* will prove to be a huge help in raising up children to be men and women who will both lead fruitful lives and impact their times and cultures with the kingdom of God.

Marc A. Dupont
Mantle of Praise Ministries

RAISING
Spiritual
CHILDREN

PATRICIA & GREG MAPES

Raising Spiritual Children: Cultivating a Revelatory Life
© 2009 Greg and Patricia Mapes

Published by Nexus Institute
P.O. Box 10277
Dayton, OH 45402
Telephone: 888-877-4248
Fax: 888-899-0284
www.nexusconnection.org

Publication and editorial services managed by Orbital Dynamics,
www.orbitaldynamics.com
Editorial manager: Lauren Stinton
Cover art by Trace Chiodo
Interior layout by Zach Mapes

ISBN: 978-0-9840767-0-3
Library of Congress Control Number: 2009928875

Printed in the United States of America.

For more information about this book or Nexus,
please visit www.nexusconnection.org or call 888.877.4248.

To Anna, Sarah, Duncan, and Zachary and Tania Mapes,
whose lives provide us immeasurable joy,
hope, and inspiration.

Contents

Acknowledgments

First and foremost, we must acknowledge our children's contribution to this work. This book would be much shorter without them, because we would know little that is valuable about families and children. We are so grateful for the strong, bright, tenacious, persistent, kind, loving, and generous people that they are. They have helped make us who we are today.

Life has been our greatest resource for this work, but there are some individuals who have made very important and specific contributions. We especially want to thank John and Paula Sandford for the inspiration they have been to us over the years and for the exceptional kindness of John with his hectic schedule not only to review the book but to write the foreword. We would also like to thank:

— Jim and Mims Driscoll, for their true friendship, honor, and integrity;

— Lauren Stinton, whose expertise and insight in editing helped drive this project and make it a much better work than what she started with;

— Mike and Kathy Campion, for their friendship, experience, professional expertise, and input into the work;

— Greg and Lela Leman, for having the courage of their convictions and for being stellar examples of godly spiritual parents;

— Sherry and Dennis Doyle, for their encouragement, decades of friendship, and for teaching Patricia things about raising sons that she had never imagined;

– Susan Stinton, who proofed the manuscript, and for all of the named and unnamed contributors of stories and anecdotes that provide wisdom and illustration for all of us; and

– All our compatriots and co-laborers who provided encouragement and more in preparation for the writing of this book: Doug and Camille Kinnell, Kraig and Sue Shaw, Lorrie and John Callaghan, Romina and James Arrington, and Emily Boe.

Foreword

Greg and Patty Mapes have written a timely book that fills a gap. Much has been written calling for mothers and fathers to be good Christian parents, but there is too little telling what to do practically to raise spiritual children. PKs and MKs (preachers' and missionaries' kids) have filled our counseling offices at Elijah House too many times because of this lack, to say nothing of the children of the general Body of Christ. Parents have too often simply not known how to transmit their faith to their children.

Paula and I know what we are talking about, from both ends. We have given prayer counseling to so many Christian families whose children's lives are in shambles. Many times that has been the result of the parents' giving the children's time and attention to religious enterprises. I did not say "Christian enterprises," because our discernment has so often been that it was not God who demanded the sacrifice of the children's time and attention, but fleshly zeal. Sometimes, demands do make it so that sacrifices have to be made, but here again, too many times such godly parents have not known how to provide quality time so that their children could feel loved and honored rather than abandoned. Children of God's servants have too often struggled with jealous anger at God, because in their eyes, it was He who took their daddies and mommies away from them. This book offers greatly needed viable antidotes.

On the other hand, Paula and I know what Greg and Patty are saying from the other end of the spectrum. Early on, the Lord said to us, "John and Paula, I have called you to pio-

neer inner healing, to be forerunners in the resurrection of the
prophetic office in the modern day, to lead into reconciliation
between people groups, such as Indians and Whites, to lead in
rediscovering the power of intercession, etc., but none of those
tasks, and not all of them together, is as important as the raising of your six children! That is your first priority in life!"

We tried, not always successfully, to remember that
admonition. We made special times for the children, inviolate by
"devil telephone." We played together and took trips together.
We involved them in the ministry with us whenever possible. We
prayed with them in and about everything. And we made sure
that they enjoyed a good, wholesome earthly life as children
before being called into ministry. I did not say "worldly life";
children need a good time growing up on the good earth before
being called into high Christian service.

By the grace of God, the result is that all six of our children know the Lord as their Savior, love, and serve Him. Our
son Tim said to us one day, "Thank you, Mom and Dad, for
modeling a Jesus we could love and accept." He was confirm-
ing our insistence that children need to experience Jesus
humanly, in the life we live with them day by day, earthly as well
as spiritually — first naturally, then spiritually. That theme is
constant throughout *Raising Spiritual Children*.

That principle (the natural first, then the spiritual) is
found in Scripture: "However, the spiritual is not first, but the
natural; then the spiritual" (1 Corinthians 15:46, NASB). We
see this in the life of our Lord Jesus Christ. Though He was
God's Son at birth, the Bible does not record any miracles
done by Him in His childhood. It does speak of His confound-
ing the scholars in the temple when He was twelve (Luke
2:46–47), but immediately thereafter, it says He went down
with his parents to Nazareth and was submissive to them and
grew in wisdom and in stature and in favor with God and man
(verses 48–52). It says nothing of Him going out to preach,
teach, or work miracles as a teen, or as a young adult. He
worked no public miracles at twenty-one or at any other time

until He was thirty years old.

What was the very Son of God doing all those years? Wasting time? Not being who He was called to be? Or was He first becoming fully human before becoming fully spiritual? He is our model. We are to become fully human and fully spiritual sons and daughters of God, in that order.

Greg and Patty have not lost sight of that simple spiritual principle. A constant refrain within this book is stories and examples about how to involve children and teens humanly and spiritually without controlling, manipulating, demanding, or taking the enterprise of discovery away by over-teaching. Too often, we have tried to make our children become too spiritual, in our fleshly zeal, before they have had a good earthly human base in their life with us as their parents. *Raising Spiritual Children* is down to earth, real, and full of common sense, as well as being spiritually keen and biblically sound.

I am honored to write this foreword, from a heart of both hurt and rejoicing. I have grieved for so many Christians devoted to God, who have not had such a book as this to keep them from devastating their children's lives. And I rejoice, because here at last is a book that can help well-meaning servants of God fulfill their first priority: the human and spiritual raising of their children unto the Lord.

Ephesians 6:4 (NASB) says, "Fathers, do not provoke your children to anger, but bring them up in the discipline and instruction of the Lord." Fathers in the world have provoked their children to anger in countless ways, but Christian fathers have done it most often by fleshly zeal that abandoned their raising. This book answers the question, "Just what is it we can do that raises children truly in the 'discipline and instruction of the Lord'?"

Don't just read the book and lay it aside. Keep it handy as a resource manual when you need to remember what to do and what not to do for your children's raising — that they may become fully human and fully spiritual sons and daughters of God.

May God bless your family as in Ephesians 3:14–19, that your family may be filled with all the fullness of God, growing in the love that surpasses knowledge, so that you and your children may be rooted and grounded in the love of God for Him and by Him as their very real and loving heavenly Father.

John Loren Sandford
Founder, Elijah House Ministries, Inc.

Preface

Fifteen years ago in the middle of the night, our house burned to the ground. Greg and our youngest child, Anna, were badly injured. We spent months traveling back and forth from the hospital for their rehabilitation.

One day I was chatting in the car with Anna. She had been amazing during this very difficult time. Burn injuries are traumatic and painful, and the treatment is equally harsh. During the hours and hours of treatments she endured, little Anna would pray and call out to Jesus. Now the worst was past, and we were pulling the pieces of our lives back together.

That day in the car I asked my daughter, "What do you think about everything that happened with the fire?"

Anna was only eight years old at the time — a very quiet and often shy little girl. She looked out the window and told me, "At least no one will ever be able to say that I'm not brave."

It broke my heart to think that a little eight-year-old would have to be brave. At the same time, however, I knew in my spirit that this was an invaluable revelation Anna had had about herself, and that God would call upon that courage in the future.

In Numbers 13, courage was what separated Joshua and Caleb from their comrades. It was what enabled them to say, "Yes, we can take the land," when the other men with them reported, "This is never going to work." Love is the most important virtue (1 Corinthians 13), but we often need courage to do the things that love requires. Unfortunately, many of us don't fully understand what true courage is. The house fire had taught our daughter something at eight years old that many people go their entire lives without learning.

And that is the purpose of this book. After thirty years of child rearing, ministry involvement, and prophetic training, we've come to realize the importance of learning certain principles while you're young. If you can grasp them as a child, you will save yourself potentially years of hardship and pain as an adult. A firm understanding of these principles smoothes the road, highlights the path to your destiny, carries you forward, and brings you honor and favor with God and humanity. With these things hidden in your heart, you *will* succeed, and we trust and pray that this book will help you and your family get there.

Our Most Important Actions As Parents

At some point, all parents face anxiety, exasperation, and perhaps even fear — fear that our children will fail, that we will fail our children, that one or the other of us will look bad. When Greg and I arrived at this juncture, we looked for parenting books on this topic of raising spiritual children and didn't find any. We sought out assistance from other parents and pastors in our sphere, with little or no useful help to be found. We knew we needed help, but we didn't know where to look for it. There are resources for adults who want to grow in their character and spirituality but very few to be found for parents who want to help their children do the same. We were hard pressed in our quest and for the most part came up empty-handed.

Titus 2 talks about the older women who could teach the younger women. Twenty years ago, my good friend Sue Frisbie and I (Patricia) looked hard for these women. We wanted to find the mothers and grandmothers who could teach us how to raise our children the way that we felt God intended.

But then one night, I had a dream in which the Lord told me, "You two are 'it.' You are the women of Titus 2." Obviously, we were not exclusively the women of Titus 2 for our generation, but for our season in that place, we were what God had provided.

This was such discouraging news that it woke me up! I immediately thought, *That wasn't God. Did we have pizza for dinner?*

In the morning when I was more coherent, I realized it had been the Lord, but I didn't understand how it could be true. I called my friend Sue, and immediately she told me she had something to tell me. From her tone, it didn't sound like good news.

"God spoke to me in a dream last night," she said. "He told me that we were the women of Titus 2."

We were so discouraged! We knew we didn't have the answers we were looking for. We wanted insight, help, correction, revelation, *information* — we wanted a model for the kind of mothers we should be. The only possible qualification we had was that we were slightly older than most of the women around us, but that, clearly, wasn't the kind of qualification we were looking for!

Almost three decades have passed since then, and we still don't have all the answers; however, we've realized the two most important things we could do as parents: We can grow our children's character and validate their relationship with God, from whom their spirits came and their gifts were given. Character and gifting are two key components for fruitful Christian living. In order to mature spiritually, we cannot have one without the other.

About This Book

As you read this book, please keep a few things in mind. First, this book specifically addresses the issues of spiritual life and spiritual gifts. Although it does speak to many aspects of parenting, it is not meant to be an all-inclusive parenting book. For a comprehensive parenting guide, we strongly recommend *Restoring the Christian Family* by John Loren and Paula Sandford (originally published by Victory House Publishers, 1979).

Second, if you sought out this book because you're frustrated and feel completely "in over your head," be at peace. God gave these children to you, and so from that, you can extrapolate that you are the best person on Earth to raise them. Like us, you may not have all the answers, but if you can be consistent and operate in love, demonstrate mercy, and walk in faith, you are on your way to finishing well. And so are they.

Finally, this book was originally written for parents of young children (up to about thirteen years of age), but the principles found within it apply to every child — those who seem to possess strong revelatory gifting as well as those who are gifted in other areas. As we go through this book, these are our assumptions:

- God still heals, moves, and speaks to His people today;
- All children, some in particular, have spiritual gifting (this differs from natural gifting such as musical talent); and
- Dreams and visions from God are significant and worth searching out.

While teaching and sharing on the topics in this book, we have discovered that children are not the only beneficiaries. Parents are finding release and freedom, and grandparents are realizing that they have more to give than ever. Pastors, leaders, and mentors will recognize that these same principles apply not only to their birth children but also to those who are their children by the Spirit.

Thank you for picking this up. We trust it will be beneficial to you.

Chapter 1

Character: The Foundation of Spiritual Living

What you see and hear depends a good deal on where you are standing; it also depends on what kind of a person you are.
— C.S. Lewis[1]

An irony of parenthood is that most of us embark on this journey of child rearing with less preparation than we put into a family vacation or a move across town.

If we are going on a three-week road trip from Newark to San Diego, most of us don't simply pile into the car and head west; we sit down and systematically plan a three-week trip. We look at the maps. We consider the season. How many nights will we be staying in hotels? How much fuel will we need? Will the tires be good for the whole trip, or do we need to replace them now? What do we need to pack? What will we do when we get there?

If this level of planning is necessary just for a family vacation, how much more is needed for the family itself? The latter "journey" will last much longer than three weeks and will require more than we could ever fit into a suitcase. Most children will eat at least 1,095 meals every year. Multiply that times eighteen years, and you have 19,710 meals you are responsi-

1 Lewis, *The Magician's Nephew,* Chapter 10. See Bibliography and Suggested Resources for more information.

ble for — per child.

Have you considered this? But more importantly, have you considered how you will use those meals to nurture not just your children's physical well-being but also their spiritual well-being? How in the world are you supposed to do this, let alone be successful doing it?

When Greg and I first embarked on this journey, it didn't really occur to us how unequipped we were. We had our fair share of misinformation, too. Most of our friends who spoke with authority on the subject didn't actually have kids. We were swamped with information from all sides, and for years, the result was self-condemnation and guilt; we thought we just weren't doing it right. We suffered from what our good friend Dr. Michael Campion calls "analysis paralysis": We had no grid with which to process the vast amounts of (sometimes conflicting) input we were receiving, and consequently, we had no idea how to proceed. Finally, we realized that when it came to other people's advice, we were allowed to pick and choose. Although most people had good intentions, their advice wasn't always helpful, and we didn't have to accept it if we didn't want to. Family, friends, and mentors may be worth listening to, but afterward you alone can assess their helpfulness. At the end of the day, you are the leader of your home, and you must set the course for your family.

After realizing the above, I (Patricia) began to realize something else. I wanted to see how well we were doing with my extensive, decades-long child-rearing plan, and God surprised me. "You don't have eighteen years to raise your children," He said. "You have about ten to twelve years per child to sow, invest, and impart in significant measure. Then you will have four to six years before you see what will germinate."

I slowly began to understand what the Lord was saying to me. Until children are ten or twelve years old, they are subject to our controls and boundaries and are limited in resources to what we give them. By far, we are their primary source for input, correction, love, and assets. If their behavior doesn't meet with our liking, we can substantially modify it, using the control we have over them.

But by itself, this is not enough, because great men and women of God must have more than modified behavior. We cannot get our children to their destinies. No matter what our children are gifted in, their gifts will not get them to their destinies. What will help them get there? Their character. As parents, this is one of the most important things we could understand. When our focus is on helping form our children into great men and women of God who know who they are and that they are loved, everything else, including what they have been called to do, will fall into place.

That is the tricky part. If we are not careful in the ten to twelve years we have to nurture, teach, and train our children, we may train them simply to respond a certain way to certain stimuli, and that's all. True character is much more than knowing how to behave; it involves internal transformation. In order to instill true character, we must do more than manage and modify our children's outward behavior. We must also instill integrity, courage, and godly values — internal issues of eternal importance.

Children may seem to be honest, diligent, and respectful of others, but it could be that they have learned only how to have peace in their lives, be rewarded, and not rock the parental boat. That isn't character; it is behavior conformed to parents' pressure — and it is the beginning of a pattern that may encourage the children to conform to peer pressure later on.

Time and time again, we have observed many kids who seemed to be good, solid Christians and have it all together, but once removed from the constraints of home and Christian schools, they totally fell apart at college or out on their own, indulging in all manner of unsavory behaviors and failures. Not only are their parents shocked at the children's behavior, but the children are often somewhat shocked as well. They came into this increased freedom simply by growing older and subsequently found themselves in new territory and a new season or level of testing for which they were unprepared.

We must remember that this test of maturity and morality, which every child must face, is not our test. It is our children's test, and the one thing that will cause them to pass or fail is their character.

This presents an obvious question: How do you know which type of children you have? Do you have children of exemplary character, or do you have children whose behavior is exemplary only because they have deemed it their best course of action? When your twelve-year-old turns eighteen, or even sixteen, will you be encouraged by who he is? Or will you wonder how he became this person you hardly know? If the issue of character isn't worked out in childhood, it *will* hinder adulthood.

Check your children's progress as they are growing up by giving them opportunities to make decisions and choices. Be willing to take small-scale risks at home and allow your children to make poor choices with lesser consequence, so that you can understand what areas of their character need shoring up. And especially important — never, ever let your children use their spirituality or gifting to excuse wrong behavior! We'll be talking more about this in a later chapter.

If your children have soft spots in their character, the best place to discover them is under your roof, when you are there to help them. Yes, it may mean there is a little remedial work to do, but that pales in comparison to what the issues can become if they aren't discovered until the children are off to college or out on their own.

Four Foundations of Character

As parents, we are helping shape containers — not flashy and extravagant objects that others can admire, but containers that are capable of holding volume. Will these children, spiritual beings who have gifts from God, be people of depth? Will they be able to relate to the people God has called them to? Will your son have enough love to minister and bear fruit? Will he have enough honesty and integrity that people will believe him? Will your daughter have enough wisdom to know how to do what she was created to do? Will she, in turn, be able to raise spiritual children of her own? Have a healthy family?

There are four foundational aspects of children's character that are critical to the growth and development of spiritually minded adults. Those four foundations are beliefs, identity, vision, and relationships.

Beliefs

What we believe, consciously and unconsciously, can keep us from our destinies. God determines our destinies, but our beliefs determine whether or not we will reach them — even whether or not we are capable of reaching them. For example, if Samantha's destiny includes a healing ministry, but she doesn't believe God heals, she will not be able to do what God has called her to do.

In order to live full lives, our children need to understand that they are spiritual beings in a natural world, not natural beings in a natural world. Pierre Teilhard de Chardin (1881–1955), a Jesuit priest and mystic, said, "You are not a human being in search of a spiritual experience. You are a spiritual being immersed in a human experience." Our children need to grow up with this understanding — and with the realization that they are in this natural world for only the briefest part of their existence. Most of their existence will be lived in Heaven, a spiritual realm that this natural realm mirrors only darkly (1 Corinthians 13:12).

Identity

Children (as well as adults) need to have a clear sense of self in order to become who they were created to become. Gifted children are prone to identify themselves with their giftings — and they may want to glorify whatever makes them stand out in the crowd. If children don't know who they are without their gift-ings, they will become adults who have lost their true identity somewhere along the way and now relate to people only through their abilities, something that makes them unreliable, incapable of true friendships, and very susceptible to failure.

Also, when children don't know who they are, they will tend to withdraw from others every time they don't understand what God is telling or showing them. Over time, this can lead to compromise and denial of the spiritual realm. It can even close down the children's giftings or delay their destinies and character development.

When children reach this point of unreconciled realities (where what they see, know, or hear in the spiritual realm is different than what they see, know, or hear in the natural realm), they must have a clear sense of self-identity (both in the natural and the spiritual), for this will allow them to rest in that in-between space and not be drawn into confusion.

Vision
Having a dream for our lives is important. It allows us to see the road ahead and therefore traverse the course. It is very hard for our children to keep moving forward when they aren't able to sense where the path is taking them. In addition, having goals, purposes, or expectations for their lives will help keep them from becoming self-centered and grossly introverted, which are real pitfalls for spiritual and gifted people.

It isn't imperative that the vision our children have at ten years old is what they are still pursuing at twenty or thirty. It is simply important that at ten, they know they are on the way to somewhere, to being people of worth.

Relationship
After creating Adam, God said, "It is not good for man to be alone," and then created Eve to be Adam's wife. Relationship is

at the core of our existence. For children, healthy relationships are vital, especially where spirituality is concerned. If they are unable to relate to people whom they can see, touch, and hear audibly, how much more difficult will it be to sustain a relationship with their heavenly Father, who cannot always be seen, touched, and heard audibly? Healthy relationships are good indicators of children's (and adults') spiritual health, for they demonstrate that the children are able to care about other people and can function in a community, as we all are called to do (Romans 12:5).

Character is measured by what we do, not just what we say. If our children are strong in these four foundations of character, we can rest assured that they are on the path to success.

Character and Gifting
God's gifts are given without remission. As Romans 11:29 says, "For God's gifts and his call can never be withdrawn." This means that a lack of character does not equal a lack of spiritual gifting and that spiritual gifting does not attest to godly character.

Perhaps you know men and women who have incredible gifts and are used by God in dramatic, often miraculous ways, and yet they don't have healthy relationships. Sometimes, they seem to offer more hype than hope, and their supporters don't honor who these people are apart from their gifts. Spiritual and gifted people without integrity and godly character are often temperamental and hard to deal with — and not just as children. Their lack of true character hinders the power of God in their lives. Although they appear to be "somebody," in reality they fall short of who they were created to be. We have had much experience with people who sound wonderful in public but are vicious and abusive in private.

Amazing giftings produce very little lasting fruit when their possessors have not matured in godly character. Demonstrations of extraordinary gifting may seem very impressive in the moment, but few lives are genuinely changed by them. This is but one reason that character is so important.

Something to Ponder

What Does Danger Mean to You?

The difficulty of raising children who have courage is that in order to learn to be courageous, they must experience facing and overcoming challenges, threats, and enemies.

This is contrary to everything we as parents are naturally made of. In the face of danger, we want to step in front of our children and take the "bullet" for them, so to speak. However, whatever problem this solves in the moment, it doesn't always cultivate courageous hearts within them.

David didn't just suddenly become a man of courage when he encountered Goliath. Before he fought Goliath, he had spent years fighting the lion and the bear.

I (Patricia) suspect that when David encountered the lion, he didn't think, *Ha! A lion has come to help me learn about becoming courageous.* I don't think he thought that. I'm picturing something more along the lines of, *God, help!* I bet that if his father had stepped in to deal with the lion in his stead, David would still have become a great man, but he would have been deprived of something very valuable. The lion really was David's learning lesson for the day.

When the bear came later, I don't believe that even then, David thought, *Oh, now I get it. God is helping me learn courage.* Probably it was something more like, *Aren't there any other shepherds out in these hills? Why me?*

I think David finally began to understand the purpose of the lion and the bear the day he saw Goliath. He knew he was brave because he had dealt with the creatures that had come to attack him and his flock. Therefore, he knew he could afflict the giant. Other people saw a big giant, but David saw a big target.[1]

It takes wisdom to know when to intervene and when to be one hundred percent behind our children while letting them step up to the challenge themselves. I would encourage you that the pain you may feel today by not making everything "right" will pale in comparison to tomorrow's pain if your children are unable to make good decisions, live lives of peace instead of fear, and make right choices on their own.

Learn to stop and consider the conflicts your children are having. Is this something they might be able to navigate? Remember, life prepares us for more life; by interfering today, are you depriving your children of lessons that will bear great fruit tomorrow?

Whether we are talking about relational issues, physical challenges, emotional discomfort, or something else, raising children often means stepping back to let them grow. If your children want to cross the creek by balancing on the rocks, and you think they will fall, what is the downside of that?

1. They get wet.
2. They may scrape a knee or an elbow.
3. The current is so strong that they will probably die.

Short of the third possibility, we encourage you to give your children the greater gift. Let them learn to do more than they have ever done before. The day will come when all of you will be grateful.

Be wise and don't deprive your children of their history. As David said in 1 Samuel 17:37, "The LORD who rescued me from the claws of the lion and the bear will rescue me from this Philistine!"

---

1 Paraphrased from Dutch Sheets

Chapter 2

Nurturing Your Children's Identities

Jane and her family moved halfway across the country when her girls were eleven and thirteen. They were moving before school started, and every fall they had the tradition of going shopping together to buy new school outfits. Jessie and Joanna wanted to go shopping for their new outfits before they moved. Being the practical mom, Jane suggested the girls wait until after the move so that they would know what the girls at their new school were wearing. But her daughters disagreed.

"I think we should just go and buy what we like," Jessie said, "and they can copy us if they want to."

This is one of my (Patricia's) favorite stories. Jessie and Joanna knew who they were; they had a strong sense of self. As they went through middle school and high school, they often stood out from the crowd — not because they were outlandish or rebellious, but because they were at peace with who they were. They had many good friends and were well liked by their teachers, but they were also capable of making up their minds for themselves and pursuing what interested them even if it meant doing so alone.

How do we develop within our children a strong sense of identity — the unshakeable core that defines who they are, what they want in life, and why they do what they do? When our children know who they are, they are able to be different from their peers and follow God even when He leads them to do great, remarkable, potentially risky things that have never been done before.

As parents, there are three important things we can do to help our children develop their own unique identities. We will discuss each of these in greater detail as we go through this chapter.

First, in order for our children to discover who they are, it can be very helpful for them to discover who they aren't. We can purposefully arrange for them to interact and spend time with people of different ages, personalities, and preferences, with our appropriate participation.

Second, our children can't be told who they are supposed to be or what they're supposed to do with their lives. We can assist them on this journey of discovery, but we can't compel them to do or be what we feel they should do or be; they need to discover their destinies for themselves.

Finally, we need to let them explore their desires and find out what they like and dislike without fear of failure or disapproval.

The Importance of Diversity

Small children have a very limited sense of identity, much of which is attached to their parents. For the first several months, they cry when their mother leaves the room because she is their world; without her, they feel lost because she is who they are. As they grow older, however, they naturally become more aware of themselves as individuals. They begin to understand that when Mom is in the kitchen and they are in the living room, everything is all right; their world doesn't fall to pieces. They begin to see themselves as separate entities.

Much of the Western World has lost sight of how children naturally develop, and we no longer recognize certain childhood milestones. For instance, beginning around the age of two, most children learn to use the word "no." They are not being rebellious; they are recognizing that they are individuals and therefore have the power to refuse. They are individuating and defining who they are: "I am here, and you are there." This is an important step for children developmentally, and we should never tell our small children that they are not allowed to tell us, "No."

Of course, this doesn't mean that there aren't any consequences for that reply. If they say, "No," to something they normally desire, like ice cream, don't give them ice cream anyway. If they say, "No," to bedtime, acknowledge their desire, but let them know that it is time for bed and then put them there. If they refuse to pick up their toys, assess an appropriate discipline. The goal is to allow them to declare their individual person; it is not to allow them to rule the house.

Again, we cannot take their assertions of "no" as rebellion. Only when children truly recognize who they are as individuals can they wholly and generously give themselves to others.

Our children's understanding of who they are is vital to their growth. *There are three Sams in my class,* a little boy may think, *but I am the only Samuel Winston Brown.* As simple as this seems, this type of thinking helps him differentiate himself from the group and recognize his own uniqueness and self. A strong sense of identity allows children to make independent choices and decisions, while a poor sense of identity creates problems that worsen as the children grow into adulthood.

The first problem a weak sense of identity creates is that the children tend to identify themselves more strongly with their environments and daily routines. When their circumstances ask them, "Who are you?" they reply, "This is what I do; therefore, this is who I am. I am a second grader." Or, "I am Joe's friend." They identify themselves based on their relationships to things or other people. There is an absence of their innate sense of self, and thus they don't know how to define themselves in any other way.

We can see evidence of this in everyday encounters. Years ago, we took a tour group to Israel. It was a great time in many regards, and most of the group enjoyed the experience; however, two teenage girls did not. They nearly starved one day before we broke down and found a place to buy them hamburgers and French fries.

It was somewhat frustrating. Every morning, the hotel served a huge buffet. There were rolls, hard and soft cheeses, hardboiled eggs, fruit, yogurt, and a variety of other delectable foods that were common to the States. The issue was that in middle-class suburban America, where these girls were from, the foods were served at different times of the day. You didn't eat certain things for breakfast, so these girls didn't eat. They wanted bacon and eggs for breakfast; fruit for snacks; and pizza, burgers, and fries the rest of the time. They weren't willing to take risks as small as trying different foods at different times of the day.

This may seem like an insignificant thing, but it reflects their insecurity in themselves and their identification by external circumstances. It reflects "I am what I do" or "I am who I know" rather than "I am me." If children have a strong sense of self, they will be much more able to explore, have adventures, and experiment with new things. Those words, especially *experiment*, have recently developed negative connotations in the Western World, but when tempered by God's truth and morality, they are very positive. They are what allow creativity and innovative processes to develop. They are the incubator for courage, creativity, and perseverance.

Children who don't know who they are have a hard time "getting out of the box." A strong sense of identity built on a foundation of basic security will allow children to try new things, experiment with their likes and dislikes, and become more involved in other people's lives. Why? Simply because they know who they are, which means that even if their adventure doesn't go as they expect, they won't lose themselves in the process, be injured beyond repair, or have substantial regrets. Another way to say this is that a strong sense of identity brings freedom. When children are free to make choices and decisions based on who they are and where they want to go in life, greater vistas are opened to them.

Hand in hand with the first problem caused by a lack of self-identity, the second problem is that children will then need someone or something to tell them who they are. As children, that "someone" is often their friends at school. Peer-group thinking (the wants and decisions of the group as a whole) tends to gravitate to lower denominators and typically doesn't instill any sense of individual accomplishment. It is risk-averse and inadvertently opposes anything that would make one of its members stand up or out from the group. The group itself may take incredible risks (bullying, drugs, alcohol, sexual promiscuity), but it doesn't allow for individuality.

In addition to affecting mindsets and behavior, peer-group thinking also affects our children's spirituality, for peer groups are very rooted in the natural realm. They can stifle spiritual awareness and openness and may lead to the children's eventual denial of their spiritual gifts. This is prone to happen because, in order to be accepted by the group, the children will need to do what makes sense to the group, and spiritual giftings don't always follow human rationality (Isaiah 55:8).

When Moses sent the twelve to spy out the land God had clearly promised them, only Joshua and Caleb were sound in their thinking — they were willing to take risks and do what God had told them to do even though, by all natural accounts, the battle was going to be daunting (Numbers 13). The other ten absolutely refused, and it brought judgment on the entire nation. Every member of the group had the same experiences and witnessed the same things, but Joshua and Caleb put their attention on the positive (the bounty and fruit in the land), and the rest of the group focused on the negative (the obstacles). Joshua and Caleb believed that God could overcome the roadblocks; the rest of the group did not. This is the first exploit in Scripture involving the two men, so we can assume that they lived relatively normal lives until this point, but they had been allowed to grow in courage and relationship with God. The result was that peer-group thinking did not affect them.

God usually speaks to individuals. Even when He is

speaking the same thing to many people, He most often speaks to them one at a time. This is another reason peer-group thinking is not easily influenced by spiritual matters. If our children are more in tune with the group than with who they are as individuals, they will not be much in tune with God and what He is saying to them personally.

As parents, we can measure our children's sense of identity by asking certain questions. Does Sam really like only ketchup on his hot dog, or does he just think he does because his best friend, Joe, eats his hot dog like that? Does he believe that he needs to be like Joe in order to be Joe's friend? Typically, these aren't conscious thoughts for children, but if we explore these ideas with them, our children will probably be able to articulate answers for us. Sharing preferences is normal among friends, but it shouldn't happen at the expense of children having their own very sound, very secure identity.

What is the opposite of peer-group thinking? What will help our children discover who they are more quickly and easily than anything else? One of the greatest ways children can discover their individual identity is by being around people who are distinctly different than they are.

Greg and I homeschooled our children for many years, and though we're not advocating homeschooling in this book, that method of education does enable children to grow up without age-segregated peer groups. In most traditional school settings, children are divided into predefined groups: fifth graders, third graders, senior class, etc. The members of these groups tend to view members of other groups as either above or below them; the younger children may not be worth their time, and the older children may be "stuck up" and not want them around. They then learn to gravitate to their own age group, and this is where peer-group thinking comes into play.

Homeschooled children, however, can move up or down the age scale much more readily and don't strongly label themselves "fifth grader" or "ten-year-old," because at home it doesn't matter. Most of them grow up with siblings who are different ages, and they may spend nearly as much time with adults as they do with other children. This helps them relate well to all age groups.

Aside from homeschooling, you can achieve similar results by encouraging your children in activities or groups that are not age sorted. For example, they could volunteer at a local nursing home or farm, help out with a fruit stand, work in the church nursery, join a young adult's ministry team at church, or take part in other activities that attract people of different ages. Also, you can make a conscious effort to spend time with families who have younger or older children, perhaps having a game night once a week or participating in other activities with them. If you would like certain adults to be role models for your family, facilitate relationships with them that include your children. These might be something strictly social, like inviting them over to your house for dinner, or it might include outings to sporting events, etc.

When our children have diverse groups of friends and acquaintances, they will become more and more aware of themselves as individuals. They will also grow more comfortable interacting with people in general, which is imperative for all of their relationships and occupations in the future.

Let Them Discover Their Destinies Themselves

As a child, Lizzie loved to make people laugh, but her quiet, rather reserved parents didn't think she was humorous. In fact, they appeared bored and sometimes even a little bit revolted when she played around with them. So Lizzie, the budding performer, assumed that being outgoing was somehow wrong, and as she entered her teenage years, she decided to become an accountant like her father. She was an intelligent, capable woman, so even though she wasn't doing what God had created her to do, she was very successful at it. But deep inside, she felt that something was missing.

Although her parents loved her very much, they inadvertently kept her from being who God had created her to be

— a funny, joyous child who wasn't entirely like them. They had not been open to her interests and desires, which consequently taught her that certain parts of her — the parts that would have brought her life — were to be disdained. Today her parents don't understand how she couldn't be happy, because she has been successful in the same things they were successful in — the only things they hold to be valuable.

Jake wanted to grow up and be in a band. Even as a teenager, he was an excellent musician; he was obviously gifted, and everyone who heard his music praised him. But his parents knew that many aspiring musicians aren't overly successful. Have you heard the joke about the only difference between a musician and a large pizza? The punch line is that a pizza can feed a family of four. Jake's parents wanted him to have a good job and be able to take care of his family, and so they expected him to go to college instead of doing what he'd always wanted to do. So he went to college, started a band, and then dropped out of school. Time has passed, and he now calls his parents only on birthdays and Christmas, because every time they talk, he is reminded of how disappointed they are in him. His lifelong dream has become a reality, but they don't see it that way.

The residue of rejection or disdain remains in children long after their awareness of the original issue has faded. Good and well-meaning parents are often totally unaware of what they did to cause their adult children's unhappiness. As adults, these children may not be able to recall where or when the unhappiness began, but they do know that somewhere within them, something isn't as it should be.

As parents, we greatly desire for our children to succeed, but it is sometimes easy for us to forget that God, not us, determines at what point they become successful. Many of our common parenting and schooling techniques focus more on children *conforming* than discovering their uniqueness — which is the opposite of what God intends. He didn't mean for children to be miniature versions of other people; He created them to be themselves.

Our position should be to love, provide, train, and guide our children, so that they can become what they feel led to become. Periodically we should take a time-out to examine our interactions with them. How are we molding them? Do we validate only what we personally appreciate? For example, are A's more valuable when they are in math or science but not other courses? We need to be guides for our children, but we can't be the Director. If their interests are met with our disinterest, dismissal, disdain, anger, impatience, or distress, our children may eventually go a different direction and give up searching for the pearl of great price that God had planned for them to find.

If we discover our children's destinies "for them," when they reach adulthood, they will eventually have to locate and dismantle all the enforced aspects of the "destinies" we helped them find. Their sense of identity may resemble what God desires for them, but it will lack certain foundations of character that are necessary for their continued development. Not only this, but their healing process may need to include releasing resentment and frustration and forgiving us, the interferers, as well.

Some of us have spent half our lives pursuing others' dreams for us. The result is that we are cranky, slightly jaded, somewhat ineffective people. Like Lizzie, some of us have perfected the art of performing life, but we don't know a thing about the art of active living. Now adults in our thirties, forties, and older, many of us still talk about "finding" ourselves. We can't quite seem to pinpoint who we are, though we don't have any trouble knowing who we "should be." Perhaps this is why midlife crises are so common in our culture; we didn't discover who we were as children, and we're trying to answer that question now.

Growing up is meant to happen when you're a child. It is a much more painful and distressing experience to grow up as an adult. We know scores of individuals today who are in jobs, marriages, and situations they don't particularly care for, simply because they were raised to respond to the cues of their parents and others. On the surface, their character doesn't seem to be lacking, but internally they have no idea who they are, which often results in diminished commitment, vision, and/or hope.

Think about it like this: A gardener spends considerably more time caring for and feeding a new tree than he does a mature oak. The new tree needs additional care so that its roots can grow deep into the soil. In some cases, it also may need to be staked and strung so that the trunk will grow tall and straight. Eventually all those tethers come down; most individual care ceases; and now, established and capable of taking care of itself, the oak will grow on its own while the gardener puts his attention elsewhere. Children are much the same. When they are small, they need us for almost everything, but as they become established, they are capable of choosing for themselves which "branches" go where.

Spiritual children will see God in many places, occasions, and objects. They will see God in His creation — the wind, sky, and music will all speak to them if we don't train it out of them. As our children grow, we must trust God and know that He who made Heaven and Earth, as well as our children, knows what He is doing. We need to let their life adventures be our adventures to watch, not direct. We should give them the values and understanding they need to be successful, but then we need to let them develop their strong sense of self and who God made them to be.

Here is the truth of the matter: If our children hear from God and are in relationship with Him (and we cannot be the judge of those relationships), we can conclude that they are on the right path; they are doing what God has for them to do. He is a capable Guide, and we are simply our children's caretakers for a finite number of years. Our role is to support their ever-increasing independence, not enforce our boundaries on who and what they become.

This calls for wisdom and humility on our part, and it leads us to the final point.

Let Them Unearth Their Desires

Oak trees drop thousands of acorns a year, but only a few of those acorns actually succeed in becoming trees. There is no evidence that this is oak tree failure, acorn failure, or that God made a mistake when He created oak trees and acorns. He made the trees to reproduce, and so amongst thousands of acorns, only a handful need to follow through and successfully germinate. The principle is the same with our children's interests and quests — which, we might add, have much better prospects than a handful of acorns.

When we allow our children to experiment with their likes, dislikes, hopes, and dreams, we not only help them find who and what they want to be, but we also help them avoid uttering, "If only . . ." later in life.

The next step in this is training them not to fear risk and failure. A child who begs to play the clarinet in the school band and then gives it up shortly thereafter is not a failure — she has just successfully discovered that she doesn't like playing the clarinet. How much better is that than the forty-seven-year-old computer programmer who still thinks she would have loved playing the clarinet, but her parents ignored or dismissed the opportunity? As we talked about in the last chapter, when our children are ten years old, the nature of the vision is not nearly as important as the fact that they have one.

When we say this, we do not mean that every desire to cross our children's minds should be pursued. Nor do we mean that you should try to afford, either in time or money, everything your children might want to try. Depending on the children, that could be nearly impossible!

When playing the clarinet, joining the swim team, and learning to fly airplanes all come up at the same time, assess what you can afford time- and money-wise, and invite your children into the decision-making process. This helps them decide what is truly important to them, and it completely eliminates any feeling of rejection or deprivation. They will be able to conclude, *I had to choose between these things, and I picked the clarinet.* This process helps them define who they are and what their priorities will be. We need to use our discernment; listen to God; and then, if we need to say, "No," or think God is saying, "No," we can communicate that in a way that doesn't imply that the desire is wrong, foolish, or "not God." In this, however, be very careful that you don't use God to justify what you simply don't want to do. Be sure to mirror His heart and His will accurately to your children — a topic we will be discussing in more detail later on.

As we raise our children to love the Lord and be aware of the spiritual realm, we need to watch for what delights them. What gives them joy? What do they have passion for? And then we need to take everything in stride. They don't need to be starting their life vocations now, so don't worry if they are currently interested in activities that don't seem suited to them. Not every little boy who wants to play football is called to be a professional football player. Not every little girl who takes flutes lessons will pursue the instrument through college. These things will work themselves out. In the meantime, your children will be exploring, stretching themselves, setting goals, making friends, and experiencing the satisfaction of belonging to something bigger than they are.

Almost every activity has the potential to impart important spiritual truths, even if it is pursued only for a time. For instance, sports can impart a great deal of spiritual understanding: teamwork, leadership, courage, commitment, and more. Music is inherently spiritual, as are most artistic endeavors. When we distill them down to the basics, mathematics and science are essentially the study of creation. The Lord told Patricia once that there is a mathematical formula for the creation of the universe — and that it could be played musically. What could be more spiritual than that?

Athletics, artistic pursuits, and analytical professions are not contradictions to spiritual lives. If our obviously spiritual or revelatory-gifted children want to be musicians or teachers instead of ministers, encourage them. Have you ever met a pastor who isn't called to be a pastor? We have. It can be a painful experience for everyone involved.

As our children grow, some of their interests will evolve, and others will be left behind. Whether the interest changes or the child changes doesn't matter. The important thing, as we have mentioned, is that children don't see themselves as failures. Our efforts and projects sometimes fall apart or cease to hold our interest, but that should never cause us to think we are failures, though something may have indeed failed.

Failure is a normal part of life — one that many of us try to sweep under the rug. We quickly forget how many successful people had to experience years of failure before they experienced success. For example, Sam Walton (founder of Walmart) suffered multiple business failures and bankruptcies before he became one of the most successful businessmen in America. Thomas Edison tried to create the light bulb more times than anyone could count — but he never gave up hope, and eventually he succeeded. Failure teaches a lesson that can't be learned anywhere else: It isn't fatal!

Is it possible that without experiencing failure, we won't be able to truly value some great successes? Consider all the celebrities in our culture — actors and athletes who demonstrated great talent as children and then were often raised without ever knowing failure. The world is at their beck and call, but their lives often are disasters. Children who have never experienced conflicts or failures don't know how to survive when life becomes difficult. Children who have never had problems can think problems are the end of the world.

When your children announce their ever-changing occupational goals, encourage them to pursue their interests. Fear of failure is the enemy's weapon. Every child's life should include some things that fall short, because without them, he or she is ill-equipped to do what is required to achieve success.

Raising Your Children's Identity in God

A friend of ours, Andrea Bariether, recently told us a story about her son, Aaron. When he was five, Aaron came home from an outing with his dad and told her that he had heard God's voice. As she questioned him about it, she realized that it hadn't been a strong thought or impression; he had heard the audible voice of God in his ear. God had told him two things — one, that Aaron was smart, and two, that they were going to move out of their house. They had no intention of moving at the time, but they did move exactly three years later. They moved to *Aaron* Street. And to top it off, the side street was Benjamin Street, which is Aaron's middle name.

"It was great confirmation that we had moved to the right place!" Andrea said.

It also plainly demonstrated to Aaron that God was speaking to him, that he was able to recognize God's voice, and that he was smart! It was quite a revelation to understand that three years before his family had even thought of moving to another house, God was preparing the perfect place for them. Clearly, nothing happens without God's knowing.

A strong sense of identity also enables our children to explore spiritual matters. They (as well as their parents) don't have to be concerned with becoming lost or losing their bearings in this exploration, because they know who they are. In other words, their sense of identity allows them to enter into a deeper knowledge of God and His identity.

Again, our children are spiritual beings having natural experiences. Not only are they our sons and daughters, but they are the children of God as well. They belong to Him, too. As they grow in their sense of belonging to God, their awareness of Him and of spiritual things will often increase exponentially. They will then reach a critical point in which they move from knowing Him as the God of their mother and father to knowing Him as *their* God. Their relationship with Him becomes personal and real.

Our son Duncan was about fourteen years old when he

and I (Patricia) went to a conference together. It was a good evening meeting. The young adults and teens were especially moved during worship, and when we got home Friday night, everyone was charged up. Duncan said his watch had stopped at 7:10 p.m., right after worship had begun. It was a new watch, and it shouldn't have broken, which made us think it could be somewhat significant. Duncan was sure that God had a message for him.

One of the ways that God speaks to us from Scripture is by giving us numbers in pictures, dreams, or visions (see the numbers section in Chapter 9). When we pick up on these clues, we can search out what God might be saying. That night, we did what we always do when we think God has given us a reference — we looked for 7:10s in the Bible. We looked in Isaiah, Jeremiah, Proverbs, and the psalms, but nothing seemed to stand out to us. It was late, and we all needed our rest. I told Duncan that he probably would figure out what it meant tomorrow.

That night, we had the house fire. The building essentially erupted and burned to the ground. It was a horrible, devastating event that left Greg and the girls badly injured and the house a total loss.

As you may imagine, chaos doesn't adequately describe the next hours. Later that morning, Duncan found someone to take him from the hospital to the house. Many people were there from the church. They wandered around, looking for anything they could salvage, praying, not knowing what to do. Duncan started walking through what remained. Everything was wet from the firefighters' efforts and from the following rain. It smelled, and it was sad.

Slogging through the muck, Duncan kept saying to no one in particular, "I feel like Job. I feel just like Job." Suddenly he remembered — 7:10. Someone got him a Bible, and he looked up Job 7:10, which read, "He shall never return to his house" (NKJV).

Duncan came back to the hospital to find me. He needed to know what that meant. I didn't know what to tell him other than, "God knows."

One thing I did know, however. From my perspective, that day Duncan moved from worshiping his parents' God to worshiping his God. He has never wavered from that. It wasn't that he hadn't known God before — God had spoken to him even as a boy. But in my opinion, that was the day he came into his own adult relationship between him and God.

Relationships are organic in that they grow and change over time. Sometimes good friends become better friends, and sometimes they drift apart. As our children grow up, part of forming their own sense of identity includes developing a relationship with God, one that is personal for them. They can't rely on our experiences with God forever; they need to have experiences with Him for themselves. Then when they go to Him in prayer or repentance, it won't be a vicarious relationship but a real relationship that is tangible for them.

If their own, personal relationship with God doesn't develop in childhood, it won't magically appear when the children reach adulthood. Some years ago, I (Patricia) was visiting with a pastor's wife. The daughter of a national church leader overseas, she was married to a passionate minister and seemed to be a very strong believer.

We were talking about kids, and I shared this concept with her. After a while, she stopped talking, and I asked her if she was all right. In the middle of our conversation, she had realized that even though she was a grown woman, probably around thirty years old, she had never made that transition. She had lived in this country for ten years and was happily married, but she had sensed an instability in her life that she had never been able to put her finger on. That day she discovered what it was, and it changed her.

Thus began a process of going to God and acknowledging that she was not coming as her parents' daughter but as herself, submitting anew to Him with the understanding that He was *her* heavenly Father. I don't know how long that process took, but I don't think it was laborious. Afterward, she became a stronger woman and a leader in her own right, because she had fully embraced her own relationship with God as her Father.

In Conclusion

How do we develop a strong sense of identity within our children?

We need to let them interact and spend time with people of different ages, personalities, and preferences.

We can't tell them what they should do or be. We can help them on the journey to discovery, but they need to realize their destinies themselves.

We should let them explore their desires and find out what they like and dislike without fear of failure or harsh correction.

Also, we need to remember that children aren't chattel — we don't own them. Too often, moms and dads offer their children's time and help without recognizing how much this diminishes the children and treats them as if they are possessions. Obviously, this is not the parents' intent, but it can be the result. However, when we give them the opportunity to say, "No," we are showing them respect and are affirming who they are as individuals. This is vital to their proper growth and development. Once children recognize who they are, they can more easily give themselves wholly and generously to others.

If our homes are safe havens for our children — places where they know that they matter, that they are important even when they misbehave, that they are still loved and accepted even when they fail — then they will be prepared for life. They won't be afraid to take risks because they will know that even if they fail, it won't destroy them. They may be embarrassed on the short term, but they will know that they are successful people overall, even if they didn't succeed today.

Something to Ponder

The Power of "Why?"

Minds are like parachutes: They only function when they're open.
— Lord Thomas Robert Dewar

All of us have probably heard about the benefits of having an "open mind." *Simple enough,* we may think, but how do we nurture open minds in our children?

One of the evidences of cultic thinking is that everyone must think alike. Even we as Christians occasionally strongly resist the idea of openness. (Often we do this out of fear or anxiety.) Many well-meaning people gradually end up believing, *We can be friends only if you think the same way I think.*

Christian thinking, however, should be as boundless and open as the universe God has placed us in. God has given us this Earth, and we need to discover it. A child with an open mind will have the eyes to see, both in the spiritual and in the natural. A closed mind sees only what it already knows and what is agreed upon, but an open mind can see what is possible, what is hidden, and what isn't yet . . . but could be.

Steps to Nurturing Children's Minds:
1. Give responses that leave room for exploration. If your young children look at a donkey and call it a horse, don't automatically correct them and leave it at that. Instead, ask them about the

features of the donkey and the features of a horse. Talk about the similarities and differences. See if they can "discover" that what they thought was a horse is really something else.

2. Hand in hand with this, be open to discussing their mistakes. There are a lot of ways to refute an answer without shutting your children down by telling them, "You're wrong." One of the simplest ways to let children know they are mistaken is to ask, "Why?" Why did they think it was all right to drop algebra before discussing it with you? Why did they think it was all righ to stop at the park and play ball with Billy after school before coming home and checking in or asking permis sion first?

3. Remember that in spite of the age we live in, the process of discovery is often more important than merely knowing the end result. Over the years, there have been plenty of four-year-olds who couldn't tell the difference between a donkey and a horse, and yet they eventually went on to attend Harvard or Oxford. In life, it is more important to be able to discern, think, draw sound conclusions, and make good decisions than it is to be able to spout out facts.

4. Encourage your children to think about more than just them-selves. We simply reiterate the rules when we tell children that they need to ask permission before playing with friends after school. With appropriate consequences, they will learn. However, the better lesson is for them to understand the rea-sons behind the rules. They need to learn that they don't live in a vacuum; they are not the center of the universe, and what they do impacts other people as well. For instance, their choices often impact you, the parent. If your children are old enough to walk to school, they are also old enough to have learned that you love them and are concerned with their welfare.

The best thinking happens when children have open minds and spirits. If Joey checks in after school because he knows his parents are waiting for him, that is not just a lesson learned or a rule accepted; it is an expression of kindness and maturity that will open him to blessing and favor throughout his life. It is fine to have a rule, but the rule should be the backup for good thinking.

Jesus said in Matthew 7:13: "'You can enter God's Kingdom only through the narrow gate. The highway to hell is broad, and its gate is wide for the many who choose that way.'"

Have rules ever led anyone to God's narrow gate? It is often repeated, "Rules are made to be broken." If we have a rule, we can also justify compromising the rule, and compromise won't get anyone to the narrow gate. Children need spirits that are open to God and nurtured by family and others in order to make the right choices in the right moments, all along the way.

Chapter 3

You and Your Identity

The question isn't, "Were you challenged?" The question is, "Were you changed?"
— Leonard Ravenhill

"**I** am not sure how to start," our friend Camille wrote to us. She has four children. Each of them is uniquely different in personality and in how he or she sees God. Camille wouldn't call her family incredibly gifted or anointed; they just love God and try to pursue Him in all that they do.

Dylan is Camille's oldest. As a child, he loved to worship God and had an amazing ability to bring people to Him. At three or four years old, he would share stories of Jesus with all who would listen. Camille's non-Christian friends would call him the "little preacher boy."

But then in 1995, little Dylan was diagnosed with leukemia. The treatment was harsh, intrusive, and arduous. Camille's entire family felt like they were dreaming and would wake up at any moment. She remembers sitting at the hospital and wondering, *How am I going to do this? Where is God in all of this?* Dylan was looking to his parents to help him through this difficult time, but they didn't have a single answer to give him. Camille and her husband, Doug, were completely depressed and consumed with the fear of losing their firstborn, while struggling to make a normal life for their other children.

One day, Camille was sitting on the couch crying, and

Dylan came up to her. He looked at her and said, "Mama, you know that if I die, I live forever."

It was such a simple statement, but something happened in his mother's heart. She realized that she had missed a truth that her six-year-old had understood. He had a better grasp on the kingdom of God and who God is than she, and from that moment on, Camille knew she needed to embrace how God thinks and not how circumstances dictate. They needed to trust Him and what He said, not the doctors and what the doctors said. She knew Dylan was going to live, no matter what that looked like to her, and she needed to search out and teach that to him in a greater way.

Beginning that day, Camille and Doug sought to show Dylan what trusting in God means on a daily basis. They started with practical things, such as living a normal life. They had been living in fear — fear of him dying, of him playing with other children and catching a common cold. They had been told to limit his interactions because of the disease, but they began to rise above it when they let him live a normal life.

Not everything came to them right away, Camille told us; it started in baby steps that became huge steps later on. They no longer lived in fear of Dylan's death. They no longer kept friends and family away. They played when they wanted to and went to the park and did normal things that normal families would do. And every time they did something together, they would pray and tell the kids how good God is and how He heals and moves in their lives.

"I felt as if I were an outsider looking in at the miraculous," Camille said, "when all the time it was me watching us change." These little moments and actions of prayer and gratitude created an atmosphere of revelation.

And today, Dylan is a happy seventeen-year-old who is cancer free.

In order to raise spiritual children who love God with all their hearts, one of the first things we need to discuss is *you*. As parents, you cannot impart to others what you don't have. That makes it imperative, for the sake of your children, that you come to grips with your own identity so that you can help your children form theirs. As you do this, your life, your family, and your children will prosper.

We shared this story of Camille and her family because it shows so clearly how the thoughts and decisions of parents can change the course of the entire family. When Camille and Doug realized who God is and who they are in relation to Him, they were able to show their children how to live in light of those truths; the entire family was then able to live boldly, without fear. As parents, we have authority in our families. This means that when we adjust our thought processes, we will eventually see that adjustment in their thought processes as well.

What insecurities do you face now? Do you know who God says you are and respond accordingly, or are you insecure about what other people think of you? Do you see your fears more than you see hope? Are you a truly kind and generous person, or do you feel unappreciated and resent how much you do for your family? Are you still stuffing down junior high rejections, trying to prove that you really are pretty or successful? Most importantly, do you know who you are whether you succeed or fail?

All of these are identity issues, and in order for you to raise your children the way God intended, *you* have to be living the way God intended you to live. If you want your children to grow up trusting Jesus, the best way to show them how is by trusting Him yourself.

The following three steps may at first seem simplistic, but we have found them to be much easier said than done. If you can hold them and cherish them until they become second nature to you, we think you will be amazed at how your life, as well as the lives of your children, will change for the better. These three steps are:

◆ Be willing to change your mind,
◆ Realize that God knows, and
◆ Measure your life in light of eternity.

Be Willing to Change Your Mind

In Ephesians 4:23, God tells us to let the Spirit renew our thoughts and attitudes. In other words, we need to change our minds about anything that doesn't line up with God's truth. This is what Camille and Doug accomplished. They realized the errors in their thinking and sought to embrace God's thinking instead, even if they didn't fully understand and had to accept certain aspects on blind faith alone. When we are willing to lay down what we think is right in order to do, say, and become what God thinks is right, we will be the parents and people God intended us to be.

That being said, however, one of the difficulties of being human is that we do not stand still well; we leave the path. God calls us to start and remain at Genesis 1:27: "So God created human beings in His own image. In the image of God He created them; male and female he created them." Clearly, God created us and not the other way around, but unfortunately, somewhere in the twists and turns of human minds, we move to Point B, where we begin to assume that God thinks like we do, which steals our hope.

Worry is born at this latter point. Have you ever been fearful? Have you ever said, "That can't be God," only to find out later that it actually was? We were made in His image, but from the moment we draw our first breath, the carnal realm is at work in our lives, trying to conform us to its ways:

"God wouldn't do that."

"I don't see how God could have allowed that."

Have you ever considered that questions such as these are an indicator of how far we have yet to go? If God is in control of the universe (and He is), if nothing happens to us unless God allows it (and nothing does), then the better question is not "How can God do that?" but "How can I be transformed to see what God sees?"

Children tend to flow easily in the things of the Spirit because they haven't become as saturated in the world and its ways as we have. As adults, God often needs to re-teach us what we accepted without question as children. There is no condemnation in this. We simply need to change our minds.

Years ago, we were in an incredible season of God's training. I (Patricia) didn't actually know what was going on at the time. All I knew was that we had been raising our children, having a good life, and suddenly — poof! Everything changed. Greg had taken a few months off from work to help a friend start his ministry. When those months were over, Greg, who had never had to look for a job in his life, was at a loss. Nothing was working. At the same time, the Texas real-estate market, in which we were heavily invested, was crashing, and the oil and gas rules for income reporting were changing. These changes altered how our investments were treated from a tax standpoint and considerably increased our tax liabilities. All of this left us with deficits that exceeded our normal income by five to ten thousand dollars every month. To help pay the bills, Greg began doing consulting, which would have adequately covered our expenses under normal circumstances, but in our current situation, we found ourselves facing extraordinary shortfalls.

During this time, we saw God answer prayers in amazing ways. People we prayed for were being healed of all manner of illnesses and diseases. A little boy's heart was miraculously reconstructed between tests and before his surgery. Cancers were disappearing, and we were hearing incredible, faith-boosting stories. It seemed like all our prayers for others were being answered — prayers for miracles, healings, provision, and restoration.

One would think that I'd feel happy and content, but I didn't. While other people were being blessed, I didn't know from one month to the next where our provision would be coming from.

Yes, we did live in a nice house, and no one was starving, but things just kept going wrong. For instance, one day Greg received a letter from the estate of a somewhat distant relative. I thought, *Oh, good! We'll be getting some money.* The trustee, however, was writing to ask Greg to exempt himself from the inheritance. It wasn't the largest sum in the world, but the other relatives didn't think he should receive it since he was not as close to the deceased as they were.

To my amazement, Greg agreed. (Clearly, he was in a different place mentally and spiritually than I was!) I was aghast. Every month I would make a list of all the bills and expenses we were facing, and we were regularly thousands of dollars short. We could have used that money.

Months later, we came home around two in the morning from a twenty-four-hour prayer meeting. After carrying the children up to bed, I decided to go down to the mailbox. Greg protested, knowing that whatever was there at two in the morning would be there when the sun was up, but I felt such a strong urge that I quickly ran down and got the mail. Inside was a check from the estate. The other relatives had reconsidered and had unexpectedly sent Greg his share of the inheritance. It was within pennies of what we were short that month on our bills and expenses.

Awesome provision? Yes. Was I blessed? I was ecstatic! But just a few days later, I hit bottom again, unhappy and miserable and wondering how we were going to make ends meet next month.

During this time, we prayed constantly. I had declared my trust in God for His provision over and over again, and yet I needed a transforming change of mind. I had a very narrow view of how provision could come, and I was blind to anything that didn't measure up to that view. Our home life began to suffer. I didn't play with my kids like I had before. Because I was miserable, I made everyone else miserable as well.

One day, the Lord told me to put all the bills in a box and not think about the bills or talk about the bills or open the box until I either had a new bill or money to pay them. It was very difficult, but I knew it was God, so I did what He asked.

I put everything in the box. Then I grabbed the kids and off we went to the park. I knew I had to keep busy so that I didn't return to focusing on our financial trouble. And it worked. It wasn't very long before I had my life back. God was teaching me to change my mind. *Think about this, Patty. Not that.*

Philippians 4:8 (NKJV) is the key to mentally healthy living:

> *Finally, brethren, whatever things are true, whatever things are noble, whatever things are just, whatever things are pure, whatever things are lovely, whatever things are of good report, if there is any virtue and if there is anything praiseworthy — meditate on these things.*

Many of us assume this verse pertains only to lofty, highly "spiritual" topics like prayer, fasting, and other "church" matters, but it actually means everyday life things. Focus on God, not on bills that can't be paid; not on car troubles; not on bad doctor's reports; not on any worry, legitimate or otherwise. Focus on what is true, what is noble, what is pure, what is lovely, what is of good report, what is virtuous and praiseworthy. *Think about this, Patty. Not that.*

Months after packing away the bills, I opened the box and saw a notice from the electric company on the top of the stack. As you can imagine, the electric company and I had a lot of correspondence in those days, and I knew that they were people of their word. If they said the electricity was going to be shut off on a certain day, that was the day they shut it off. I started to panic when I saw the notice, because the shut-off day was twelve days earlier. I called them immediately. "I have the money. Can I have an hour to run a check over?"

The lady on the other end was very nice, but she told me that there wasn't anything she could do for the account, because the service had been disconnected.

I was sitting in an air-conditioned house with the lights on and the dryer running. Clearly, the service hadn't been disconnected.

"Please give me just an hour," I began again.

"I'm sorry," she repeated, "but the service has been disconnected."

We went back and forth a few more times before I realized what had happened. I apologized to the woman for taking her time and hung up the phone. God said to me, *Patty, you think you need money to have power, but all you need is Me.*

We can ask, "What in the world is going on here?" But that won't solve the issue. The more important question is this: "God, what do You say is going on here?" The focus makes all the difference.

"God, what do what from me today?"

"What is it You want to change in me?"

"How do You want me to respond?"

God is doing something in our lives all the time. I want to stop trying to convince Him to take up my agenda and instead have the revelation of His agenda for my life. This way, I will be able to work in concert with Him and not inadvertently oppose what He is doing. I want to hold tightly to God and His supernatural universe, holding this natural life only loosely.

A few months later, God gave me a "final exam" on this topic. Greg was in Kansas City for meetings at a church some of our friends attended and was staying over for their weekly Friday night worship service. I was home in Dallas with the boys. I had been waiting for a $10,000 check to clear the bank so that I could pay the bills.

This check was from a client who had financial issues. Sometimes he would pay us, and sometimes he wouldn't. Sometimes the checks would be good, and sometimes they wouldn't be. I had learned that *if* we received a check from this man, I should give it a week to clear. (Years ago, a check could take many days to clear.) More than a week had come and gone without incident, so I sat down, wrote all the checks I needed to write, and mailed them off.

The day after I paid our bills, the bank called. The teller and I were on a first name basis, but today she wasn't chatty. She told me that the last check I had deposited had been returned by the issuer's bank for non-sufficient funds.

I protested. It had been more than ten days since I had deposited that check! Apparently it had been returned once already, and she had redeposited it for me, because she had known how disappointed I would be. I hung up totally distraught.

All I could think about was that $10,000 of bad checks was a felony, and I was going to jail. Greg was going to worship, and I was going to jail! Crying and complaining, I told God, "Fine, just fine! I have some cash in my purse, and I'll take the boys to dinner, and then we'll die. We'll just die!" A little melodramatic in retrospect, but honest in the moment. I felt just like the widow from Zarephath, and I told God that. "We will just eat and die."

Completely overcome, it seemed that I remembered only the first part of that story:

> *So he arose and went to Zarephath. And when he came to the gate of the city, indeed a widow was there gathering sticks. And he called to her and said, "Please bring me a little water in a cup, that I may drink." And as she was going to get it, he called to her and said, "Please bring me a morsel of bread in your hand."*
>
> *So she said, "As the LORD your God lives, I do not have bread, only a handful of flour in a bin, and a little oil in a jar; and see, I am gathering a couple of sticks that I may go in and prepare it for myself and my son, that we may eat it, and die."*
> — 1 Kings 17:10–12, NKJV

As I complained to God, He replied, *Yes, Patty, you are like the widow from Zarephath. No one in your house has missed a meal. You have a home; your children are clothed, and, Patty Mapes, you even have gasoline in your car.*

I had known that God was the God of miracles. When a sick or injured person came to us for prayer, we had no answer for him or her other than God's healing, and so that is what we prayed for. I had learned to trust Him for healing, but I didn't know how to rely on Him for our provision.

> *And Elijah said to her, "Do not fear; go and do as you have said, but make me a small cake from it first, and bring it to me; and afterward make some for yourself and your son. For thus says the LORD God of Israel: 'The bin of flour shall not be used up, nor shall the jar of oil run dry, until the day the LORD sends rain on the earth.'"*
>
> *So she went away and did according to the word of Elijah; and she and he and her household ate for many days.*
> — 1 Kings 17:13–15, NKJV

God spoke to me through this story, and I sat down on the step in my living room and wept. God reminded me of how He had provided for us month after month in inexplicable, unexpected, and even miraculous ways. For two years I had experienced incredible visitations of the Lord in my circumstances, but up until that moment, I hadn't been able see them for what they were.

God wasn't having a problem providing for us. That was not the reason the provision seemed to appear at the last moment. What God wanted was to change me, to change my mind. Greg had sailed through this season with barely a wince. We were participating in many of the same things, praying together daily, and looking at the same lives, yet we were seeing our circumstances very differently. I needed to change my mind, because I didn't have enough room for God to be all He is. I had fixed my focus on the world, instead of the supernatural, and I needed to leave my narrow-minded ideas behind.

Just to conclude the story, eventually the check came through. I didn't go to jail, and everything worked out.

Realize That God Knows

> "And if God cares so wonderfully for flowers that are
> here today and thrown into the fire tomorrow, he
> will certainly care for you.
> Why do you have so little faith?
>
> "And don't be concerned about what to eat and
> what to drink. Don't worry about such things. These
> things dominate the thoughts of unbelievers all over
> the world, but your Father already knows your
> needs. Seek the Kingdom of God above all clsc, and
> **he will give you everything you need**.
> — Luke 12:28–31, emphasis ours

Greg ended up taking a position at the Kansas City church, so we packed up the family (there were four and a half of us by then); left behind our large, beautiful house; and moved into a little 800-square-foot duplex. Our Kansas City bedroom was smaller than our Dallas closet, and (no surprise here) I found myself struggling in my discontent.

One morning at church, an English minister taught about God coming and resting on us when we are in a place of contentment. The idea made sense to me, so, ever the person of logical and earthly thinking, I decided to work out a deal with God.

I suggested that if He would make my situation comfortable, then I could reach that place of contentment; I'd become a person of peace, and He could rest on me. It was a win-win situation.

But apparently, that wasn't what He had in mind. Instead, He told me, *Patty, I'm not interested in making you comfortable so that you can be content. I am interested in you becoming content in your discomfort.*

Paul talked about finding contentment in our circumstances (Philippians 4:11–12; 1 Thessalonians 5:16–18), but what does that look like?

Somewhat surprisingly, godly contentment looks like submission — one of the most difficult issues of our Christian faith. Obedience is so much easier. All it entails is following the rules. As we discussed in Chapter 1, obedience enables us to control our outward behavior and be rewarded for it, without necessarily having to change anything internally. By nature, submission is a heart issue, which makes it much more difficult to carry out. When we choose to submit to God, we are granting Him complete control over our lives, our children's lives, and everything else that even remotely affects us.

That bears repeating. *Complete control.*

When we submit to God, we are no longer in charge, which means that we don't always get what we want; it means we get what God wants — always. Sometimes the two are roughly the same. Sometimes, they aren't the same at all and it doesn't make sense why, and sometimes there is no answer for our questions other than, "God knows."

I resisted the dealings of God for years, but slowly I have come to realize that God is for me (Jeremiah 29:11), so when He and I differ in opinion, I should change my mind and join Him on His side of the issue as quickly as possible. It is not always an easy thing to do, but His plans and His way of thinking are the best for me and for my family.

How does this specifically relate to parenting? Our children learn to submit to God the same way we do. First, they need to believe that God is fully in control, and second, they need to understand that they can trust Him. Who models these two steps for them? We do — their parents. They are looking to us to show them the way.

Obviously, it is very hard to model submission when we can't trust Him, when we are not confident that God is with us and for us. In the story we related to you at the beginning of this chapter, our friends Camille and Doug had to ignore what their circumstances were saying and realize that God was absolutely in control of them and their situation. They then were able to submit to His will, and when they did that, He brought them life.

After we moved to Kansas City, we were presented with a host of questions, and we answered nearly every one the same way. "God knows." That was all I (Patricia) knew to say, because much of the time it was the only truth I was confident of!

Why did He choose to do it that way? Wouldn't another way have been easier? Why did He want them to walk through this? Why do we have to do this? We are faced with questions such as these on a daily basis, and often we cannot even begin to answer them. But we can know this: God knows. I wish I would have recognized this sooner. If we can teach our children to trust Him at an early age, the rest of their lives will be so much easier.

Finally, when we are submitted to God and the genuine desire of our hearts is to become the people He created us to be, we can assume that every good, bad, profound, or ugly thing we experience is part of His answer to that desire. Perhaps this was what Paul meant when he encouraged the Thessalonians (1 Thessalonians 5:16–18) to rejoice in their circumstances, no matter what. Everything can be a learning experience; everything can be an adventure. God is in control, and He is trustworthy. As these truths take root in who we are, we will discover that we sincerely do not have anything to fear.

Measure Your Life in Light of Eternity

When I (Patricia) was oh-so-much younger and life was simpler, I had different goals than I have today. One of my goals was to ski 150 days a year. I lived in Park City, Utah, so this goal was relatively feasible, and I learned some significant life lessons along the way.

As you might expect, the local people often skied together rather than with the tourists. Tourists were perceived as aliens whose purpose for existence was to facilitate our lifestyle (as in, no tourists would mean no ski resorts, and no ski resorts would mean no 150 days of skiing per year).

One of the things I learned while skiing consistently with the same group was that in life there are two types of people. The first type always looks good. They take the course of least resistance and consequently never fall down and rarely make visible mistakes. Their perspective is very much rooted in the here and now. We can tell this because they never look bad. That is left to the second type of people — the ones who are well acquainted with bad-looking moments. They are willing to look a little shaky now in order to look better in the future. The first type is never sore, never hurt, and never bruised in body or pride. They are also never better, or if they are, the improvement occurs very, very slowly. At the end of the year, all of us bruised-up, banged-up people were better skiers, while all of the perfect-looking, never-stretched, never-tested skiers hadn't really improved. Falling down isn't a problem. Not learning how to get back up — that is a problem.

An eternal perspective is the natural outcome of allowing God to change our minds and then submitting ourselves to Him and His will. When parents have an eternal perspective, we aren't discouraged by how many times we or our children fall or make mistakes; we aren't worried when circumstances don't go the way we expected. We are calmer, happier, more contented people, because we know that God has a plan, and therefore we are able to rise above the problem.

As we raise our children, we will do our best if we are training, disciplining, and encouraging them within the scope of an eternal viewpoint. I know a woman who raised five children, and the first of those children was always perfectly dressed; he looked like he had stepped out of a Gap or Bloomingdale's ad. However, by the time the fifth child was a teenager, this mom couldn't work up enough energy to care whether or not the child's socks matched. Not just matched her outfit — but matched each other!

This change in perspective applied to more than clothing as well. The last child breezed through things that the first child would never have been allowed to attempt. Was it because Mom was overwhelmed and didn't care anymore? No. Quite truthfully, she seemed less overwhelmed at the end than she had at the beginning. The difference was that in her twenty-five years of raising her children as spiritual beings, she had learned that not everything she considered important actually was important. What is the consequence of unmatched socks in eternity? Probably not much.

Can God, who holds the world in His hands, manage to uphold her home as well? As she came to the realization that yes, He could, it relaxed her and allowed her to live a healthier, more fulfilling, more peaceful life. At the end of the day, this mother chose her battles wisely. "If it doesn't impact eternity," she said, "how much should I let it impact us?"

When we begin to measure our life and our children's lives from eternity's perspective, it becomes much easier to distinguish between what genuinely matters and what doesn't. It also helps us continue and push through even when our circumstances are difficult. Without an eternal perspective, every time we encounter small obstacles, we will try to go around them, seeking to hold onto our earthly peace. We become like a meandering river: We are going somewhere, but it is unclear exactly where or if we will arrive. But if we can keep our eyes on the prize — the treasure we are storing in Heaven (Matthew 6:20) — we have a much better chance of success.

In Conclusion

As parents, our beliefs and perspectives of God and life set the course for the rest of our family. In other words, our sense of self, be it strong or weak, becomes the model for our children's sense of self. They look to us to model how life should be lived. If we desire that our children live spiritually aware lives, we must live spiritually aware lives ourselves, for our nonverbal communication speaks more than our words.

If we don't know who we are in God, it will be much harder for our children to answer that question for themselves — or worse, they will develop a skewed perspective of Him. But if we are submitted to God, know Him as our Father and our Friend, and have an intimate personal relationship with Him, our children will see these things and be able to reach for them themselves.

Something to Ponder

Love: Not a Just a Noun

Many of us have come to believe that love is something we possess, not necessarily something we do. If that is our mindset, then theoretically, the more love we feel at any given moment, the more worthy we must be as children of God.

Obviously, feeling "full of love" is not inherently bad (exempting self-love, of course, and yes, we know it is often a fine line), but we would submit to you that until we move into believing that love is a verb as much as it is a noun, our love will bear little or no fruit in our lives. If there is no fruit, how can we be certain there is really any love? As children of God, shouldn't love be constantly bubbling out of us, not in a frivolous or superficial way but in a way that makes people feel good about themselves when they are around us?

Here is a little love litmus test. You will likely come up with a grid that fits you better, but this can be a starting point:

1. When people gossip around me, I:
   a. Ignore it
   b. Join in
   c. Speak up on behalf of the person being gossiped about

2. When my disorganized friend or relative is stressed and behind schedule, I:
   a. Point out the merits of prioritizing

      b. Grow impatient because I now have to wait
      c. Volunteer to help

3. When I'm standing in the slow line at the store, and I realize that the woman behind me is running late, I:
      a. Wonder why she would stand in the slow line when she's already late
      b. Feel sorry for myself because I have so much to do (but at least I'm not running late!)
      c. Offer the woman behind me my space in line

Talk about love with your kids: what it is, what it can do for people, how much they deserve it, and how much others deserve it. Real love has legs, arms, and a voice. It covers all, but only if we offer it. Today, make your love a verb.

Most important of all, continue to show deep love for each other, for love covers a multitude of sins.
— 1 Peter 4:8

Chapter 4

Building Good Relationships

The New Testament repeatedly refers to us as the *body* of Christ — not individuals functioning separately but individuals functioning together as a whole. God loves each of us individually, yet He also made it clear that He did not create us to be alone (Genesis 2:18).

Relationship is at the core of our existence, and the building of solid, dependable character in our children requires that they witness and participate in strong and healthy relationships. Character enables genuine relationship to take place, and relationship deepens and chisels character.

Relationships between Children and Parents

Most parents begin to feel connected with their offspring long before the baby is born. This may be especially true of mothers, and it is certainly true of God. He formed our children in the womb and knew them long before the world caught a glimpse of them.

> *"I knew you before I formed you in your mother's womb. Before you were born I set you apart and appointed you as my prophet to the nations."*
> — Jeremiah 1:5

> *"The Lord who made you and helps you says: Do not be afraid, O Jacob, my servant, O dear Israel, my chosen one."*
> — Isaiah 44:2

Seeing, hearing, and touching are the principal senses we employ to connect with other people. For a pregnant mother who cannot yet hold her baby in her arms, the connection comes in a slightly different way. Because she cannot see, hear, or touch the baby using the usual senses, she is consequently much more attuned to the baby's spirit, which is fully alert and functioning even before birth.

When Greg and I counsel expectant couples, we encourage them to build relationships with their children immediately after conception. Long before delivery, they should talk to their children, pray over them, pat and stroke them in the womb, speak life into them — and then continue these things after the babies are born, which can be difficult to do. As you probably have experienced at least once, a new baby in the house requires an immediate, rather drastic change in priorities and schedules, and during those early years when four hours of sleep a night is an act of God, it can be easy for parents to forget that they are nurturing their children's spirituality along with their physical bodies.

Your relationship (or the lack thereof) with your children has an incredible impact on their spiritual health and wholeness. It is especially critical for children who are sensitive to the Spirit — those who regularly interact with the spiritual realm and have dreams, visions, and visitations from God. Why is this? Because children who are especially sensitive to the Spirit are especially sensitive to other things as well, like narcissism, deception, fear, and other demonic ploys. The enemy will try to deaden our children's sensitivity while they are young, and their relationship with us is the key element to keeping their spiritual awareness and sense of identity safe.

There are many ways for us to cultivate our children's spirituality, but relationship is at the core of them all. Not only is relationship a foundation of their character, but their relationship with us is the model for their relationship with God. When we have a deep, intimate relationship with our children, we are showing them that they are important to us — and that they are also important to their heavenly Father. Our relationship with them is directly related to how they view their relationship with God.

Greg and I are often involved in public ministry, and one of the most prevalent needs we discern in people is in this area of relationships — they need to receive the love of God. Most people know intellectually that God loves them; they have read their Bible, heard countless sermons on the topic, etc. They know about His love, but many of them don't realize their actual need to know His love — not just know about it but receive it and experience it firsthand in their lives. Because this is true, when we tell them about God's heart for them, it is often like trying to shove cooked spaghetti through a barn wall. Their worldviews don't have room for the simplicity of the topic. *I know He loves me,* they think. *Can we move to something more important now?*

What developed this immunity to God's love? It begins with parents. Many, if not most, of us had a "head knowledge" of our parents' affection for us, but their actions did not always line up with their words. For example, tired, worn-out fathers come home from the office or factory and are surrounded by excited kids the moment they walk through the door.

"Come see the fort I built in my room!"

"Come see what the dog did to Mom's laundry hamper!"

"Come see the hole I dug!"

Most of us want to give our children time and attention, but at the end of the day, we are exhausted, and there are only a few hours before we have to go to bed and then begin the next hectic day.

So in response to our children's happy requests, we tend to say, "Let me read the paper first, then I'll come out and play catch with you." Or, "Let's finish this television show, and then we'll go out and look at the hole you dug."

Our children, even our small children, are very aware of the environment around them. When we tell them that they are important but then don't show them they are important, they can do the math. They may be important, but apparently they aren't as important as the newspaper. They might be worthy, but they must not be as worthy as a news program or a re-run of *Everybody Loves Raymond.*

Mothers often do this as well. How many times have we told little Susie that we just don't have time to talk right now? We're starting dinner, taking a nap, doing laundry. But then the phone rings, and we spend thirty minutes talking to Michelle down the street. Susie has just learned that she might be wonderful and she might be special, but apparently she's not as wonderful and special as Michelle — whom she has heard us say we can barely tolerate sometimes.

We adore our children and would gladly give our lives to save them, but without realizing it, many of us communicate on a daily basis, "Give me a minute to do this more important activity first, and then we'll fill the spare time with you." Many times, our parents inadvertently did this to us, and we in turn inadvertently do it to our children, more out of reflex or lack of awareness than anything else.

This is one reason that, in general, the Western World has such a hard time trusting God's love. We learned from our role models at an early age that parental figures — of which God is one — mean what they say . . . but not always to the point where they are willing to act upon it.

"I know that God *could* heal this man, but I don't know that He *will.*"

"If I know that God is with me, why is this still so hard for me to accept?"

"I know He loves me. What's next?"

Once again, our relationship with our children is the foundation for their relationships with God.

Does this mean that we need to be at our children's beck and call? That when they ask us to do something with them, we need to drop what we're doing and attend to their every whim? Not at all. This is simply a caution not to send mixed messages.

Most likely, none of you has all day, every day, to spend with your children, but the length of time you have available is not as important as what you do with this time. What matters is that you show them over and over again that they are important and valuable. If they see you make time for them in your life, sometimes even preferring them (and your spouse) over your hobbies or friends, they will know what it means to be loved, and they will be secure in that love.

Handling an influx of playtime requests doesn't have to be difficult. If we need to say, "No," to playing dolls or slaying dragons before dinner, we should make a little play date to put the dolls to bed or save the castle together after dinner. It takes longer to justify how busy we are than it does to share an activity for a few minutes.

When requests come, we need to take a moment to reflect, to think before we answer, and then respond with love and care. How does God pursue us? That is how we should pursue our children. We need to meet them where they are when we can. It won't always be this way, and some day we will probably wish we could rewind the clock and live these years with them over again. Time is short, so you don't want to squander this season.

Work is not an acceptable cop-out. Providing for your children can be an expression of your love, but it is only one expression and is not sufficient enough to replace your more valuable relational expression. Engage your children, listen to them, and talk to them. Make them a priority. Then your children will be able to believe and trust you when you say you love them, and they will also be able to believe and trust when the Bible says that God loves them. All of this will happen simply because you modeled to them the Father's love. They know they are important to you, and so if you say they are important to God as well, they will believe it. It won't be something they just know in their heads; it will penetrate their spirits and be a real and supernatural truth.

No matter how old or young our children are, we need to look them in the eyes and give them our attention, which is more important than our words. They are valuable and worthy, and we tell them this with our actions.

Second, one of the best ways we can communicate their value and importance is by not waiting for them to ask for our attention. At least once a day, we should try to initiate some type of interaction with them. "Would you like a story? Do you want to go for a walk?"

Some years ago, I (Patricia) was helping lead a women's retreat, and we asked the women to describe their favorite daily activity. One of the young moms who had a full-time job described how, after dinner, she would take her three little children into her room. They would all climb on the bed with her, and she would read to them. They would laugh, hug each other, and play with one another.

I remember thinking that at eight o'clock in the evening, that would be the last thing I'd want to do! At the time, I was typically spending all day, every day, with my children — homeschooling two of them, cooking, cleaning up, and everything else. I was consistently available to affirm them, listen to them, and touch them. Twenty years later, I can remember being struck with the absolute joy on this woman's face as she described the evening activity, and I thought, *She can't wait to get home to her little kids.* She made the most of what she had, and I had a great deal of respect for her and what she was accomplishing.

My daily routine wasn't always filled with family. There came the year we had to stop homeschooling. When my girls were in the fifth and seventh grades, it became necessary for me to work outside the home. Greg and I enrolled them in the same school Duncan attended for high school. It was a good school, and they had an excellent after-school program that was well attended. Considering our circumstances, I knew we were making the best decision we could, but the first day I dropped the girls off, I cried all the way to work. In fact, I had to go the long way around so that I could regain my composure before going into the office.

I knew that our lives were changing forever. Sarah and Anna had never been schooled full-time outside our home before; Greg and I had been their only teachers, but now someone else was teaching them, enjoying their good times, and hopefully coaching them positively through the harder times. I was never going to be there for them in the same way again, and it broke my heart.

However, after a few weeks, I had a revelation. No one was suffering. The girls were making new friends and enjoying new adventures at school. At five o'clock, Duncan or I would pick them up, and then we would spend the evening together. Though our relationship no longer looked the same, it was just as strong as it had been before. The length of time we spend with our children isn't as important as what we're communicating during that time.

We need to use the time we have to be fully engaged in our children's lives. An excellent way to do this is by having dinner together at least four nights a week. This one detail is so important, in fact, that if we have to choose between sitting down to dinner together without a rush, or getting to church on time and sitting together, we should choose dinner. Greg and I know far too many parents who have told us that they don't know what went wrong with their kids. They were always engaged with them — meaning, they took them to church three or more times a week. Taking our children to church should never be confused with "doing something with our kids." Obviously, church attendance is important, but it shouldn't be considered family time, because the point of family time is giving our children our undivided attention.

A friend of mine, Sheila, had five children over a span of fifteen years. As her oldest was turning fifteen and starting high school, Sheila was nursing a baby. By ten o'clock at night, all she wanted was to go to bed and get some sleep while the baby slept.

One night Jeff, her fifteen-year-old, came out of his room just as she was straightening up to go to bed. He was animated and conversant. Fortunately for her, none of what he had to say seemed important, and she decided to say goodnight and go to bed.

But just as she was about to go, the Lord caught her, and she knew she would regret it if she went to bed just as Jeff was ready to engage her.

So she got out some chips and they chatted about school, sports, and people. Sheila recognized a pattern over the next few weeks, and she started to plan evening snacks and think about things Jeff might be interested in. Years later, she doesn't fully remember what they talked about — just that they talked. Jeff remembers as well, and his relationship with his mother, both as his parent and his friend, flourishes to this day.

Our children's relationship with us, their parents, is one of the most important they will ever have. This relationship will not be static. It will morph over time, as it should, and it is the model for whom and what our children will be as they mature. This is our God-ordained role to fulfill.

The second most important (earthly) relationships for our children are between them and their siblings and peers.

Relationships between Children
Tom and John are nearly four years apart in age, which is a substantial difference when children are young. A toy belonging to a seven-year-old can easily be destroyed by three-year-old hands. When the boys were small, some form of contention was an everyday occurrence.

Multiple times, a friend told Tom and John's mother, "This is what boys do, Joan. They get dirty, mad at each other, take each other down, and roughhouse. It's what they do."

For years Tom was bigger than John, although not by much. His real advantage was his quickness. Joan always knew that one day John would get the better of his brother, and that day — much to her relief — finally came. They had one last headlock, one last boy pinned to the ground, one last wrestling match. Joan walked into the kitchen to find fifteen-year-old John standing in the middle of the room, holding his eighteen-year-old brother upside down. With great exasperation, Joan firmly told him to put his brother down, which he did — not very gently and more or less on his head, but no real damage was done.

After that, John never seemed to be treated in the same little-brother way again.

While contention and disagreements are not the things of parents' dreams, they are normal. Boys become men; girls become women; and they need to know how to deal with other people, work out their differences, and stay together even though they don't always agree or like each other at times. They also need to figure out that the one with the leverage today may not be the one with the leverage tomorrow, and that doesn't have to affect who they are as individuals.

Keys to a truly fruitful life include not getting our way, learning how to overcome frustration, dealing with someone else's anger toward us, disappointing ourselves or another person, and then learning how to grow in relationship even in the midst of these potential setbacks. If we can learn how to solve conflict and resolve differences as children, we will save our families and ourselves much grief later on.

Short of serious physical injury or emotional scarring, we should let our children work out their differences. Yes, that can sometimes mean our homes experience dirt, roughhousing, and physical contact, but these small sacrifices will be worth it. If they can find resolution with their siblings, they will also be able to find it with teachers, adults, older kids, and younger kids.

Attempting to have a "grown-up" type of peace in our homes, many of us compel our offspring to relate to their siblings in a "grown-up" type of way. This usually does solve the immediate problem (the noise level, for example), but it doesn't help our children form their own relationships with one another. If we consistently intervene in our children's conflicts or disputes with their siblings and friends (as well as their teachers and other adults), their relationships are then formed through us. They don't learn to relate to others; instead, they learn how to relate to us, which leads to a distortion of our relationship with them and hinders them from learning in early years how to respond and overcome challenges in a healthy way.

In the long run, our intervention deprives them of important and rewarding relationships with some of the most important people in their lives — their brothers and sisters. One sign of a healthy family is that the children enjoy the parents' company but don't have to have it in order for them to enjoy one another. If all your children have in common relationally is you, the lack of relationship will be apparent whenever you are absent. Misguided control of our children's relationships can hinder their ability as adults to have healthy relationships.

One important life principle is that we never know who our friends are until we have been through some tough times with them. We need to give our children the gift of knowing who they are and who their brothers and sisters are — that they are people with whom they might not always agree, but ones who will be there for them even when they have disputes.

As difficult as it can be at times, when our children are in a spat with one another, be it with siblings or peers, as parents, the best response is typically the least response. Children are naturally so much better at dealing with disputes than adults are. We've all watched our children have arguments with their playmates, storm away, and announce to us that they will never play with so-and-so again. Then the very next day, there they go together, yesterday's dispute forgotten.

When they forget, we should forget. When we get involved and take on our children's offenses, we have taken on an offense that really has no mechanism for resolution. Billy and his best buddy, Joey, will eventually make up, but what will we do if we are still offended at little Joey? Are we going to go to him and try to work through our offense with him? He won't know what we're talking about. *How can you be offended?* he'll wonder. He doesn't even talk to us.

Decide in advance to let your children resolve their own conflicts, both with one another and with their friends. It can be painful in the moment, yes, but it is extremely fruitful and not nearly as painful as the alternative.

The Importance of Modeling Conflict

A friend of ours had "perfect" parents. They never seemed to disagree or have opposing opinions at all. Of course, this wasn't really true — they just never disagreed about anything in front of their children. As a result, our friend grew up thinking that arguments don't happen in healthy marriages. The first time he and his wife had a fight, he started packing his suitcase, assuming their marriage was over.

For a while, his wife didn't have a clue as to why they were having trouble in their marriage. She hadn't had the chance to meet her father-in-law before his death and therefore wasn't aware of how her in-laws had (or in this case, *hadn't*) interacted in front of their kids. When she finally realized that her husband didn't have any background in conflict management, they were able to correct their marriage's downward spiral. Our friend needed to learn that conflict and disagreement aren't the death toll of relationship — they are a natural part of life.

We submit to you that one of the reasons some people live in abusive relationships or fear of failure is that they have never learned how to process disagreements and frustrations with others. Just as we model unconditional love for our children, we need to model conflict management as well. Obviously, not all disagreements should be had in front of children, but they can learn important lessons from seeing their parents lovingly disagree with one another. Sometimes even agreeing to disagree isn't a bad solution, as long as we can keep a good share of the emphasis on the "agreeing" part. We need to let our children see that good things can come from disagreements and let them learn how to confront in love and respect those who have hurt them.

In Conclusion

Our home should be a refuge for our children, a safe house. The world can be a harsh place — perhaps it needs to be in order to work in us what God is doing. But in any case, our children need to have a place where they matter, where they are valuable, where they are loved — whether they are awkward or coordinated, musical or tone deaf, smart or mentally challenged, handsome or homely.

If we can do only so much, we need to do the part that only we can do. Let the schools oversee the academics, the coaches the sports, and the employers the work habits, but we must be the parents because there is no one else who will do that part. We probably won't be as cool as some other parents; we might not be as successful, as affluent, or as powerful as someone else, but ten or twenty years from now, none of that will matter. We will have a strong relationship with our children, and that relationship will exist forever. Our children will be able to grow up with the context and capacity for intimate, fruitful relationship with God.

Something to Ponder

More Is Not Better

More is not always better for the same reasons that *faster* isn't always better.

We in the West live in the greatest abundance humanity has ever known. In the United States, people living below the poverty line often lead lives that far exceed those of impoverished people in many other places in the world. However, surrounded by this abundance, many of us tend to waste time we don't have to spend money we often can't afford for things we don't need.

Do you fall into this category? Test yourself by looking around your house. Do you have a good place for everything? Are things put away neatly in a bedroom dresser drawer, closet, or cabinet, or are they stuffed in a corner somewhere or in a plastic bin that you're pretending is furniture? Do you have clothes, kitchen things, sport gear, or décor items that haven't seen the light of day for months, if not years? Have you ever moved to a larger house so that you could *try* to put everything away, explaining to others that you had "outgrown" your old house? Did you really outgrow your old house, or did your accumulation of stuff outgrow your old house? Do your children equate new "stuff" with approval?

Aside from the obvious reasons this is problematic, there is another important reason we would be well served to take a wiser and more simplistic approach to "stuff": The time we spend acquiring and maintaining all this excess keeps us tied to our culture's materialistic ways and leaves us less time, energy, and even interest in the people around us, especially our children.

Wouldn't it be great to give your children a better life and save money in the process? We think it would.

What Can You Do to Find More Time for Your Family?

1. Today, begin to clean out your house. You may want to start in your own closet, but if you are like most of us, you will find it easier to start with your children's closets! The one-year rule is still very effective: If they haven't worn it in a year, out it goes. You can do this with socks that don't have matches, clothing that doesn't fit or isn't needed, and items that are broken or have something wrong with them.

2. Don't buy on impulse. If you are going to the mall or sporting goods store to "see what you need," you probably don't need it.

3. Determine what your real requirements are. How many outfits do children actually need? How many pairs of shoes? How many backpacks, purses, and playthings? The answers to these questions should not be determined by what other children have. Those "other children" should not be in charge at your house.

4. Give your children boundaries, such as six school outfits and two pairs of shoes. Then let them decide which six outfits and which two pairs of shoes they simply have to have. (We moms love school uniforms, don't we?)

After tackling the closets, there is the kitchen, the basement, the garage . . . If we can reduce the quantity of stuff and bring order to the rest of the stuff, we will uncover a greater sense of peace in our homes. A real benefit of less materialism is that we will be able to take back control of our lives.

The world and its materialistic ways will always war against our spiritual lives, but we can prevail. None of us will lament on our deathbeds that we should have spent more time shopping or spending money.

Let what is valuable to you and your family determine where your resources go, especially your resource of time. If you don't, the world will be more than happy to fill the void. You will end up too busy, too stressed, or too behind to give your children what they really need from you: connection.

Chapter 5

The Importance of Consequences

"People are like stained-glass windows. They sparkle and shine when the sun is out, but when the darkness sets in, their true beauty is revealed only if there is a light from within."
— Elisabeth Kubler-Ross

As parents, one of the most difficult things we will ever face is our children's pain. It can be so heartbreaking, in fact, that many of us attempt to keep them from ever being hurt. We fight for them when they've been rejected, get them out of trouble with their teachers and other adults, and steer them away from peers who don't think they're as wonderful as we do.

In the last chapter, we discussed the importance of allowing our children to work through their differences without our interference. In this chapter, we're going to discuss how vital it is that they are allowed to experience the consequences of their actions.

Our choices and decisions in life produce results, whether good or bad. Many of us have arrived at adulthood with an incomplete understanding of this, for our parents did what we tend to do now — they spared us from relationships and situations that would cause us hurt. As a result, many of us are learning now as adults what we could have learned as children, and the bitter sting is much worse. We'll be sharing specific examples of this as we go through the chapter.

Our children's character is the measuring rod of their success. Strong character is formed in several different ways, but one of the best ways is also the most painful: suffering the consequences of their actions and mindsets.

The formation of character requires consequences. Picture your child playing on the beach. If she digs a hole in the sand and fills it with water, what happens? At first the water will be fairly pure salt water, but before long, it will start mixing with the sand. Even though the hole is filled, the water isn't pure, and after a while, the murky liquid seeps away altogether, leaving only the hole.

What turns sand into something strong and solid that can hold and keep water? A furnace. When a glass blower shapes and fires sand in high heat, the sand can be transformed into a vessel capable of holding anything. Liquid isn't going to seep out the edges, nor is the glass going to dissolve away as the tide comes in. In fact, if we have a lid for our new glass container, we can take our pure water and go anywhere we want with it.

Our children's character is the vessel that contains their spirituality and gifts. These vessels need to be of the highest quality possible so that their gifts can have the greatest (most fruitful) impact. The furnace is the only way for this transformation to happen.

If we protect our children from the potentially painful experiences they need to have in order to mature, they will never be able to "hold water." Worst of all, they will be frequently controlled, driven, or motivated by fear; they will lack courage.

Don't Deprive Them of Consequences

The laws of physics state that every action has an equal and opposite reaction, and the same is true of our lives. Our positive conduct, behavior, and communications have positive consequences. Likewise, negative behavior begets negative consequences, and it becomes worse with time. Whatever lesson seems painful at four, eight, or twelve years of age will be much harder to learn at twenty-four or forty-four. Not only will it be more painful, but it will be more humiliating as well. Children tend to be more resilient than teenagers and adults.

We are the leaders of our homes; we can decide for ourselves whether or not we need to spank our children or if we want to use time-outs, groundings, or some other method of discipline. (We'll be talking more about discipline in the next chapter.) But whatever we do, we must not deprive our children of their consequences, because that will ruin them.

Gabe's mother cannot bear for her son to feel bad or rejected, so whenever difficulties arise, she tells him, "Don't let this bother you, because you are much more important than that other person." She thinks that if Gabe feels like he's better than the people who reject or say mean things about him, the sting won't be as severe — and it isn't. Gabe's mother is successful in her mission.

However, she has no idea what will grow from this seed she is planting. The real reason Gabe isn't always invited to his friends' parties and play dates is that he doesn't share well. Of course, he isn't aware of this character flaw, so, based on his mother's comments, he assumes he's being rejected because he's better than everybody else and they know it. He is growing up without learning how to interact with others, let alone be sensitive to their needs and desires. If he never develops relationally, he will likely be handicapped in many aspects of adult life.

Along the same vein, little Missy needs to learn that she can't be the princess every time she and Bella get together. Bella gets tired when she can't be anything but the servant, and play dates with Missy and Bella usually end with one or both girls in tears.

Missy's parents could decide to withdraw her from that relationship in order to protect her from Bella's enmity, but Missy needs to learn how to be a friend now, not later when it could cost her a job or even her marriage. They must not protect her to the extent that she grows up thinking other people exist to make her happy. The only thing worse than being five and alone is being thirty-five and alone. What is unpleasant at eight can be a disaster at twenty-eight, thirty-eight, or older.

How Missy's parents respond to this situation will affect Bella as well, because she also has something to learn in this relationship. She needs to learn that it is all right to say, "No." If playing with Missy means that she must always be the servant and she doesn't like it, she needs to do something about that.

Erroneous thinking as children sets us up for few friend-ships and limited influence later in life. Unless grace intervenes, when Gabe is fifty, he will still be gifted and valuable, but he will have a hard time keeping close friends. He'll continue to assume that he's being rejected because he's special, not because he's hard to deal with. Missy, ever the princess, won't be able to relax unless her husband and children are following her orders, and Bella will run herself dry thinking it's her responsibility to keep her friends and family happy.

All of this can be avoided if Gabe, Missy, and Bella are allowed to work through their issues as children. If these shortcomings are presented to them in helpful, loving ways, they and their parents can work to change flawed mindsets and behaviors.

The lack of facing consequences can be seen again and again in both Christian and secular circles. We knew a distin-guished minister we'll call Bill who was very engaging, pleasant, and never at a loss for words. But without realizing what he was doing, he effectively shut down every large social gathering he attended. He would take over conversations and direct them toward himself and what God was doing through him.

People were genuinely interested in his ministry, but that wasn't all they were interested in. So, after a while, his min-istry staff began to get together in small groups instead of larg-er, more celebratory gatherings, because if everyone were invit-ed, Bill would have to be invited, and then no matter whose birthday or what holiday it was, the party would turn into a meeting about Bill and his ministry.

The source of this discomfort, Bill would be mortified at this description — much more mortified than he would have been if this particular character weakness had been dealt with when he was five years old, or even ten or fifteen years old. At fifty-five, there was no one around who was willing to pay the price of helping him make an effort to change.

As parents, it is not our job to make a way for our children; it is our job to equip them for the way God has set before them. We are to love them, care for them, train (discipline) them, equip them, and educate them. But we are not to forge their way, interface in all their relationships, speak for them when they should speak for themselves, or decide for them when they should be deciding on their own.

Make no mistake — this is difficult. When we know our children are about to err, it is all we can do not to intervene, whether they're four or five and having a fight with a neighborhood friend, or if they're in high school and dating someone who doesn't treat them well. We know it's going to cause them pain, and we want to spare them that. Once or twice, our involvement may not cause any damage; however, if we don't allow them to realize the gravity of their decisions, they won't be able to grow up in those specific areas.

Please don't misunderstand us in this. We're not saying parents should never help their children. There is a substantial difference between ERRORS (big mistakes that take years to recover from) and errors (small mistakes that will quickly pass). In most cases, if we can spare them the former, we should. But the latter errors, the small mistakes, are learning experiences that can produce the fruit of wisdom and understanding in young lives.

Big errors — what parents fear most — usually don't happen overnight; they come through openings that were created when the consequences of the little errors weren't experienced. If we have trained our children well, they won't get very close to the big errors, because the small errors will have taught them all they need to know.

When Zachary, our firstborn, came along, we had close friends whose firstborn was about a year older. They came to the job of parenting more qualified than we did, at least on paper — he has a Ph.D. and she is a professional administrator. They read every book available on raising children, which worked to our advantage because that kept them at least one step ahead of us.

They were very generous with all of their books, manuals, etc., since they were always finishing what we were beginning. At first, I (Patricia) assumed their generosity was because they were being thoughtful, but as the years wore on and our parenting styles became more and more divergent, I realized that their generosity masked their concern for our children and the "flawed way" we were bringing them up.

As parents, we were very different. We believed that at times children needed to be spanked; they did not. We didn't believe that children should be able to talk to adults in a rude way; they felt that children shouldn't be stifled. We felt that children should understand that they were not adults; my friends thought that children should be treated the same as adults.

So there we were: two little boys who loved to play together and four adults who frequently had great difficulty coping with their differences.

When our friends' son, Curtis, was about six years old, all of us went on an outing together with some other friends. Curtis had had enough grownup fun for one day, and he wanted to go do something else. In keeping with his understanding that his input carried the same weight as everyone else's, he hauled off in his brand new, very pointed cowboy boots and let his father have it right in the shin. And in keeping with their parenting style, his dad didn't really respond. However, his face contorted in the most unnatural way.

I felt bad for him, though perhaps a little vindicated. I was also more than a little concerned for Curtis. How would he learn to play with others and have friends? We had seen things that gave us pause and for the most part no longer allowed the boys to play together unsupervised.

Eventually, we moved away and had less contact over the years. My friends put their son in school — first a hand-picked private school, then public school. By the time Curtis was about twelve, I noticed an amazing thing. He had become a very pleasant young boy. He still related to his parents in somewhat the same way (although in a more socially acceptable form), but he related well to other kids and adults, and we enjoyed having him around.

Although there was no good way to ask the question, I gathered that over time, two things had occurred. First, Curtis' parents had come to a place in their lives and careers where they simply didn't have time to keep running down to the school and helping the teacher "understand" how special Curtis was. My friends had been wrapped up in their exceptional child for many years. When new vistas opened up for both of them, Curtis had to fend for himself. Although we're certainly not advocating making family a lower priority than career, in this situation it helped them dial back their unhealthy, painstaking involvement in his life.

Secondly, it became evident to Curtis that if he wanted to have friends, he would have to be a friend; if he wanted his teachers to like him and engage with him, he would need to be likable. With no one else to fend for him, Curtis was forced to work through issues with his classmates, teachers, and others as a young teenager, and he was able to navigate those trials successfully. He discovered that relationships matter. If children (and adults) want to have friends, they cannot be grossly selfish or self-centered. However the transformation happened, it had happened for Curtis.

The next time you feel compelled to save the day for your child, stop! Even gifted children — those who shine in academics, arts, sports, or spirituality — will get their feelings hurt from time to time, and they will live through it. Painful experiences will help them grow into the brilliant men and women of God they have been created and called to be. They will learn to overcome fear, and in its place will be courage.

We know of many families in which the children's biggest complaint is that they never get away with what other kids get away with. The test of time shows that these kids were very well served by that situation, and as adults they have come to value how they were raised.

If you don't think you have enough time to deal with a behavioral issue today, think again. If you take a little time today for a small infraction, you will save many people a lot of time and pain down the road.

In Conclusion

It isn't your role to make a way for your children. Your role is to be sure that no matter how "in" or "out" of popularity your children are today, they know they are considered a valuable member of at least one group — their family. Without words, you are telling them, "You may not be part of every group, but you are an important part of this group, and therefore you are valuable."

If you have built a good foundation in your children; instilled in them integrity and character; equipped them for relationships; helped them grow in their own identities; and launched them into being mature, confident people with friends, teachers, and mentors, you will have fulfilled your role and they will turn out well. They will be strong, healthy adults who are capable, responsible, and able to do what God asks of them. This may seem like an overwhelming assignment, but it doesn't have to be. We need to grow our children's character and validate their relationship with God. These two things are the sum of all the parts.

Something to Ponder

What's Your Balance?

Writers such as Stephen Covey use the illustration of a bank account when talking about the importance of encouraging and supporting others. Some writers use the expression "affirmation account." Whatever the language, the principle remains the same.

We are continuously making deposits or withdrawals in the "accounts" we are close to: our children, our parents, our teachers, our siblings. We need to affirm our children ten times more than we correct them. As our children get older, affirmation continues to be very important. College and careers come with their own sets of challenges and rejection. We won't always be able to make daily deposits into our children's accounts, but no matter how frequently or infrequently those deposits are made, they build up and create positive change.

Children who grow into adulthood with full "bank accounts" will have "interest payments" added to them: "deposits" that bear fruit. In other words, the deposits we have made will end up increasing the value of their accounts overall.

There is transforming power in our words, and children (as well as adults) come to see themselves as the people they are being declared to be. Encouragement and affirmation bring life, but when children hear over and over again that they are stupid, rebellious, sloppy, or some other negative thing, that produces change as well. When the time comes and our children are out on their own, whatever deposits or withdrawals we made with them will still be doing their job.

How Can You Deposit Life into Your Children's Accounts?

1. Pray daily for your children that they would become who God created them to become.

2. Speak your unconditional love and affirmation over your children every day. If they are no longer living at home, email, text, write letters, or telephone them — but send your message.

3. Remember that our children are the recipients of more input/information on an hourly basis than any other generation in any time, ever. Be sure that your input makes its mark as well.

Chapter 6

Discipline: Crime and Punishment

Seven-year-old Todd is an extremely intelligent, tender little boy, and he's very spiritually gifted. He has filled several dream journals all by himself, and he's only in the second grade.

Todd recently wrote a note to a younger friend of his. The second grade class had been studying letter writing, and Todd had been paying good attention. The note was very well written, with the author's name and address at the top followed by the date, a polite greeting, and then the closing with the author's name again.

Unfortunately, the body of this well-written letter contained the following sentence: "Bring me candy tomorrow or I will kill you." The five-year-old recipient of the letter couldn't read it, so he handed it to his ten-year-old sister while they were waiting in the line for the bus after school. The sister spontaneously handed the note to a teacher, and it was all "off to the races." The teacher, who knew both boys and recognized that there was no real threat, was still compelled by school regulations to give the note to the principal. All the parents involved were alerted, and young Todd was unceremoniously and indefinitely suspended.

We all knew that Todd was a kind, loving, generous child who sincerely cared for his friend. However, there was no disputing that he had clearly threatened the younger boy. Schools, of course, have unmistakable rules about threats. Shocking and almost unbelievable violence has been inflicted by school children not too much older than Todd. Often those acts were preceded by warnings that no one took seriously, which is the reason the current regulations exist.

Todd was out of school for weeks while all the adults involved determined whether it was safe to let him return. Not surprisingly, the main holdouts weren't the parents but the administrators, who didn't have hands-on experience with these two children.

To their credit, Todd's parents maintained their self-control pretty well. Were they upset? Yes. But before they released those emotions on Todd, they took a deep breath and remembered that if they wanted Todd to learn self-control, they needed to exercise the same. So they put their own embarrassment aside and spared Todd the pain of carrying it. (Our embarrassment is not our children's responsibility, believe it or not.)

Feeling that the school was overreacting and trying to cause division between the parents, they took another deep breath and acknowledged that their relationship with this other family was their responsibility. That being the case, they could work it out in due time.

Then they walked through the problem itself. How could Todd write something like that? How could they possibly discipline him enough for all the trouble he had caused? His mother had to stay home from work for weeks. His sister still attended the school — what type of backlash would she be facing? Did they need to find another school?

In the process of seeking God and His wisdom, they discussed the problem with their older sons, who were in college but still lived at home. The older boys immediately recognized that they were partial contributors to the issue. They used the expression "I'm gonna kill you!" with their little brother all the time when they joked with him, played video games, wrestled, and goofed around. They realized how immune Todd had become to that kind of talk, and although everyone else knew what those words actually meant, to Todd they were what a boy says to his little brother when he's playing with him.

A few days into the suspension, his mother told Todd a

story about a little boy who was beaten up. The boy had died, and his mother's heart had been broken. Todd started to cry. He couldn't understand how someone could be so mean.

His mom then asked him how he thought his friend's mother had felt when she'd read Todd's note. He cried some more. "He never was going to hurt his friend," his mother told Patricia, "but it was the other boy's turn to bring candy to share and he had forgotten. He wanted to make sure he remembered the next day."

Todd was treating his friend, whom he loved, the same way his brothers who loved him treated him. He didn't have evil in his heart, but in this instance, his social skills and relational skills obviously came up very lacking.

What did his parents want for Todd? They wanted him to be a healthy young man who was kind, generous, wise, educated, and able to have friends and family with whom he functioned well. That meant two things: One, they needed to help him find better and more age-appropriate ways of expressing himself, and two, they needed to make clear to him that he was responsible for his words and their effect.

His brothers were remorseful for any part they had played in the fiasco and resolved to change their language and behavior around their younger siblings. Todd lost some privileges during a fixed time of his suspension, because his parents wanted it to be very clear that what he had done was not acceptable. Missing school, which Todd loved, was also a punishment.

After several hours of psychological evaluation and many weeks of meetings with the principal, who was becoming quite intransigent, the parents of the two boys connected on the telephone. The parents of the younger boy were having trouble balancing what Todd did with the severity of the school's punishment, as they knew that Todd wasn't actually a threat to anyone. A meeting was arranged for the two boys, both sets of parents, and the principal so that the principal could determine if the younger boy was frightened by Todd, etc.

When the meeting came, the two boys greeted each other with a great big bear hug and went off to play happily while all the adults worked through their issues.

Understanding Godly Discipline

In our opinion, Todd's parents could not have handled the situation any better. This story contains three elements that define and hold the key to godly discipline.

Love

First and foremost, his parents acted in love — real love. They never demeaned him or accused him, and they never burdened him with their own sense of shame, inconvenience, or embarrassment.

Attacking, accusing parents (those who repeatedly say things such as "I can't believe you did that" or "I'm only yelling at you because I love you") may succeed in modifying external behaviors, but they have hardened their children's souls in the process and missed many opportunities for fruitful learning. In Todd's case, there was mercy for him, even though there were consequences.

To the credit of all the parents, they were able to keep their eyes on their objectives: good outcomes for both boys and accountability for the offender. There was never any finger pointing at the other family or school, and Todd was held accountable for what he did and only what he did — which was write the threatening note. He was not held accountable for his parents' emotional reactions or career issues generated by his mother's long absence from her office.

Discovery

Second, the point of discipline is to help our children mature so that they know what to do (or what not to do) next time. While Todd's behavior was what it was, he didn't actually have in his heart or mind what the facts so clearly seemed to suggest. If we have punishment as our primary objective, we will base our conclusion on what the facts seem to prove, regardless of the actual motive behind the facts (why the child did what he did).

If Joey is wrongly punished for taking his father's tools, he learns that the system is flawed, and therefore he must learn to work the system. It also shows him that his dad doesn't trust him or believe him. If this is repeated over time, a wall may develop between Joey and his dad — one that could become permanent.

Self-control

Finally, Todd's parents were able to control their anger and shame and put off any direct questioning of Todd until they had time to assess the situation. In this case, it took a couple of days. Todd's parents understood that with a major issue such as this, they didn't need to respond hastily. They stopped, sought God, sought other counsel, and then prayerfully proceeded once they knew what their objectives were.

As a family, they re-evaluated certain things at home, and everyone was able to take responsibility for his or her part in the crisis. Todd especially. While innocent at heart, he needed to recognize the effect of his actions. He hadn't meant to cause pain, but he still had written the note, and there were consequences for that.

Also, while his parents weren't in complete agreement with the school and believed the punishment was excessive, they shared those feelings only with close friends. By keeping their thoughts on the matter private, they were able to do two things: They maintained a good working relationship with the school as the situation moved forward, and they didn't undermine their children's perception of the school administrators, who took their charge of the school very seriously. At the heart of the matter, all the parties involved wanted the school to flourish and to be a good, nurturing, successful place for education. Keeping that common goal in view, Todd's parents were able to work through any feelings of unjust treatment. They also recognized that in the long run, Todd's suspension, whether it lasted two weeks or eight weeks, did not have to impact how he felt about his school and his classmates when he returned.

Because of the way his mother addressed the situation (by telling him the story), his heart was broken rather than made defensive. Todd still had to bear the loss of certain privileges and the extended suspension, but when the situation was over, it was over. We would be surprised if the incident bears residual bad fruit for him.

When handled appropriately, godly discipline causes change and develops wisdom. It is an action of love that in turn enhances love.

Disciplining Spiritually Sensitive Children

All children seem to have a well-defined sense of justice, but spiritually gifted children — those who are particularly sensitive to the Spirit of God — are especially aware of it, and we need to consider that whenever discipline becomes necessary.

Spiritually gifted children are also spiritually aware. It will not slip past them if we are punishing them out of embarrassment, inconvenience, or anger. We model God in their young lives, and if we are punishing them for any of these reasons, they will assume that God does the same.

However, the opposite comes into play as well. If we are punishing our children because training them is our responsibility, they then will know that we are just.

Because we are imperfect beings, none of us is consistently just with our children. Therefore we need to make every effort to investigate, understand, and then act with love and mercy.

The Importance of Repentance

If we punish our children for something that we later realize they didn't do, it is vital that we go to them and apologize. Our culture frowns on that, thinking it makes us appear weak, but in this case the opposite is true. The power of apologizing and repenting to our children is immeasurable. It demonstrates to them beyond a doubt that we can be trusted, that we value them, and that we love them. It also models strength of character and humility — virtues that often aren't demonstrated very well in our time.

If we don't repent for our mistakes, our children's sense of injustice eventually becomes part of their belief systems concerning right and wrong, parental love, God's love, why they shouldn't trust people, why honesty doesn't work, etc.

None of us wants to waste our time, and raising and disciplining our children without love and mercy is not only a complete waste of time, it is destructive.

Should Each Child Be Punished the Same Way?

Punishable offenses are opportunities to guide our children through the process of growing in self-control, understanding their and others' boundaries, and moving out of the "center of the universe" perspective with which they came into the world. Because each child learns a different way, each child may require a different method or severity of discipline. For example, our son Duncan classically modeled a child who had a mind of his own. At the age of two, he figured out how to brace himself in such a way that Patricia would have to fight to pick him up off the floor. He wasn't holding on to anything, and obviously, he hadn't gained fifty pounds in two seconds. He just knew how to arch his back and distribute his weight so that if he didn't want "up," he wouldn't be "upped"! Being strong-willed, Duncan needed an occasional spanking, as did two of his other siblings.

But our daughter Anna has a different personality. The youngest in the family, she would observe what was happening with her siblings and then know what to do herself. She was a highly sensitive child, and if she did something wrong, all Patricia had to do was give her a look, and Anna would break down in tears. We didn't need to spank Anna very often, and so we didn't.

Here, we need to address the extremely vital boundaries around this issue of spanking. If you have any history of abuse (at all) in your past, eliminate spanking from your possible repertoire of disciplines. The risk of it escalating beyond acceptable boundaries is simply too great.

Further, when we say "spanking," we mean using open hands, wooden spoons, or something similar in size and weight on a child's buttocks only. Remember that you are endeavoring to get your children's attention and dispense consequence for their actions. If the action clearly requires more consequence than that of a couple of swats, spanking should not be used.

The more sensitive a child is, the more sensitive the discipline should be. Sensitivity should never be an excuse for avoiding discipline, but it is an important reason to tailor it.

Some children respond well to time-outs. When one is needed, tell your child to sit down; sit still; and get control over his or her body, mouth, or whatever it is that has gotten out of control. By being specific, you are not only stopping the wrong behavior, but you are also helping him or her to see why the action wasn't appropriate.

Depending on the child, as well as the grievance, perhaps a favorite toy needs to be taken away or a privilege denied. If Jake ran through Mrs. Smith's garden and destroyed some of her flowers, a humble apology is in order — and you can help him develop responsibility by cutting back his allowances until new flowers can be purchased for her.

Children will sometimes need help in understanding that what they did was wrong, and in those instances, writing their repentance ten, twenty, or a hundred times could be advantageous. "I am sorry that I poured soda on Sally's head." This rehearses for Josh what you hope is the truth — that he is genuinely sorry. It may not be the truth until he reaches line number seventy-five or eighty-nine, but at least he has the opportunity to get there eventually.

On a side note, if you choose to have children write sentences as a part of discipline, be sure that the sentence is a positive statement. For example, "I am sorry I poured soda on Sally's head" is a positive, repentant statement as opposed to "I was wrong" or "I was bad." You want to reinforce the positive, not the negative. "I will never _____ " sentences are also problematic since children do sometimes repeat the error of their ways. However, it is hard to go wrong when practicing repentance or repeatedly saying, "Thank you," etc.

Remember that as parents, we're not trying to change the behavior only; we are trying to change the mind. If that isn't successful, the punishment is mostly worthless. Discipline focuses on correction. A child who spills milk all over the dinner table because she was trying to be helpful may need to wipe up the mess, but she doesn't need to be punished. It was an accident. But a twelve-year-old who knocks over the milk after he's been told to stop horsing around — that is a different matter. The problem, then, isn't the spilled milk; it is that he ignored his parents' orders.

Finally, in order to effectively help our children, we need to let them know when they have damaged our trust, and then we also need to make a way for them to earn that trust back. If we don't include this latter step, we will have done more harm than good.

In Conclusion

We model God for our children, and this area of discipline is not separate from that. When disciplinary action is necessary, every step we take needs to mirror the steps God would have taken, if He were in our shoes.

First of all, love needs to coat our every action. We must not punish in anger, for that won't be lost on our children, and they will assume that God also punishes in anger. Moses was denied entrance into the Promised Land because he misrepresented God's heart to His people. We are continuously representing God to our children, and we want to remember how important God views that role.

Second, we need to discover the truth behind the facts. Why did our child do that? Was it out of spite, or was it an accident? God always understands why we do what we do; He knows our hearts, even when everyone around us assumes the worst of us.

Third, we need to exercise self-control. Our children shouldn't have to bear our embarrassment or shame. That isn't their responsibility.

What results when these three keys are correctly carried out? Hope, integrity, and courage. How we discipline our children today may turn out to be their saving grace in the years to come.

Something to Ponder

It's Never Too Late

It is never too late to "fill in the blanks" that we as parents will inevitably leave as we are raising our children.

Child-rearing is like putting together a large jigsaw puzzle. We get to the end, and we usually discover that a piece or two is missing . . . maybe even more. But here is the key: Anyone who looks at the puzzle will be able to recognize the picture, even if there are a handful of empty spaces. The puzzle still tells the story it was meant to tell.

However, should we find the missing pieces, we walk back to the table and press them into their places.

This is the way to approach our child-raising efforts. Have you realized that you made a mistake or missed an opportunity with your children when they were younger? Find a way to put that piece in place now. You may think that correcting your parenting techniques is pointless five or ten years later, but it isn't. Even if your children are thirty, forty, or fifty, they are still your sons and daughters, and it isn't too late to put all the pieces into place.

Questions:
1. Are there some things that you would like to remediate with your children? If so, write them down.

2. Take those things item by item and decide if each should be fixed by a) direct conversation with your children or b) speaking

affirmation, encouragement, or correction into their lives.

3. Put your list aside and revisit it a few days from now. As you wait, God will be faithful to bring things to mind, flesh out your memory of the past, settle your emotions about it, and give you insight and wisdom on how to proceed.

4. Create your own opportunities or take ones that present themselves to do what you decided on in Question 2. Remember that you are putting those puzzle pieces back into place one by one, and what may seem very important to you may or may not be significant to your offspring. You aren't seeking a big effect; you're just making a few finishing touches on the past.

Chapter 7

Raising Revelatory Children

Contrary to popular assumption, the word *revelation* should not be used interchangeably with *prophecy*; the two terms actually have different denotations. True prophecy is a prediction that comes true; revelation includes prophecy, but it also includes words of knowledge, divine knowings, dreams, visions, even healing, and more — it is anything that has been divinely revealed, and it isn't limited to prophecy alone.

In this chapter, we're going to be discussing raising revelatory children — children who walk in or at least stumble through the different spheres of revelation.

One of the first things we need to understand about this topic is that just as every person is gifted in one or more areas, every person also has the ability to hear God's voice and communicate with Him. This is true for children and adults alike, whether we were raised in a Christian home or not. Children often can hear God's voice more clearly than adults, because, as our son Zachary says, children don't require "unlearning" in revelatory matters. In other words, God's voice doesn't have to compete with adult reasoning.

For the purposes of this book, our definition of revelatory-gifted children denotes those who seem to exhibit a profound portion of this ability — children who have weighty dreams or visions, frequently hear God's voice, give others prophetic words or words of knowledge, and the like. Again, keep in mind that all children demonstrate these abilities at one level or another, and all children should be nurtured in them.

Second, being revelatory isn't only about receiving revelation; it's about relationship with the Father. We don't have to be in communion with God in order to have dreams or prophetic words (Acts 16:16), but to correctly *understand* a dream or prophetic word, we must have relationship with Him. We need to know Him, know about Him, and understand His ways.

Because of this, it is very important that as we raise and train our revelatory children, we focus more on relationship with God than on the revelatory gifts themselves. For our children, it needs to be a given that apart from God, their gifts are empty and unfruitful. Intimacy with Him causes our giftings to grow, and so as their relationship with Him increases, so will their understanding of their own unique giftings and how to operate in them.

How Revelatory Gifts Function

Being revelatory means that we are able, like a radio receiver, to sense or "pick up" signals from the spiritual realm. Those signals may come through impressions, senses, intuitions, mental pictures, external images, audible voices, etc. Spiritual awareness could also be described as spiritual "seeing." An example of this is the story of Elisha's spiritually blind servant:

> *When the servant of the man of God got up early the next morning and went outside, there were troops, horses, and chariots everywhere. "Oh, sir, what will we do now?" the young man cried to Elisha.*
>
> *"Don't be afraid!" Elisha told him. "For there are more on our side than on theirs!" Then Elisha prayed, "O LORD, open his eyes and let him see!" The LORD opened the young man's eyes, and when he looked up, he saw that the hillside around Elisha was filled with horses and chariots of fire.*
> — 2 Kings 6:15–17

Endeavor to raise your children with their eyes open. In other words, nurture them to see not only the natural realm but also the overlaying spiritual realm. When our eyes are open, we are aware of both realms, and we are seeing more clearly what God sees. This is important not only for understanding how revelation operates, but it also will help us better understand how to nurture our children in revelatory matters.

Some parents worry that the demonic realm will somehow intervene, and their children, who hear from God and cling to what He says, might also receive messages from the enemy. This shouldn't be a great worry. Why not? Because if they have relationship with God, they will know His voice. Jesus said this quite clearly in John 10:4–5: "'They follow him because they know his voice. They won't follow a stranger; they will run from him because they don't know his voice.'"

We want our children to be so familiar with God and His ways that they can immediately recognize the differences among revelation from God, their own thinking, or input from other sources. This comes as much through relationship as deliberate revelatory training.

Here is a good way to look at this issue: When members of bank management train a new teller, they don't spend time showing the trainee example after example of counterfeit money. Instead, they have him or her handle an abundance of real money. That way, when someone hands the teller a counterfeit bill, he or she will usually recognize right away that it is counterfeit. Tellers may not be able to say how they know it's counterfeit, but because they are so familiar with the real thing, they are able to recognize that in the midst of all this real money, one bill is counterfeit. When our children have growing relationship with God, strong character, and courage, they will usually be able to tell the difference between what God is saying and what He's not.

Unfortunately, people are not born perfect where revelatory things are concerned. Mistakes will be made. Children (and adults) can be very pure and profound in their gifting, but on occasion they can also be very "off" in what they think God is telling them. We need to recognize that all of us are in various stages of revelatory training, and with good guidance, we will grow and flourish. Mistakes are to be expected and should not be treated as disqualifiers. We need to be gracious with ourselves and others, and we shouldn't enforce what we think God is saying. Instead, we should offer it for consideration.

Along with this, we need to take care whenever we say to someone, "God says this." It may be absolutely true, but it isn't always necessary. In ancient times prophets spoke and declared, "Thus saith Jehovah," and they said that for clarity. There were false prophets declaring the words of Baal and other gods, and so the prophets were distinguishing themselves from them. Today we are not in the same kind of culture, so we typically don't need that level of clarity, especially in church or ministry settings.

Further, too often people will say, "God says," as if He appeared to them in visions and told them clearly, when this may not be the case. They may have a God-given knowing, but by definition that is not the same as God *saying* something. This doesn't mean the revelation was inaccurate at all — we just strongly believe that distinctions should be made both for the fruitfulness of the speaker and for the understanding of the hearers. There is a significant responsibility whenever we attach God's name to something. My personal preference (Patricia) is not to declare, "God says this," unless I am sure that God wants me to do so.

Again, if our children have good, strong character and are trained in this area of knowing God's voice, we as parents don't need to be afraid that they will get sucked into the New Age, become involved in a cult, or go down a wrong path. Being revelatory has the same "error rules" that apply to children in general — big errors don't happen overnight. If we train them well at this age, it will be difficult for them to choose the wrong path as adults (Proverbs 22:6).

Don't Discourage Their Gifts

Our son Zachary was still very young when Greg and I began to notice that he wasn't completely like other children his age. At four years old, he would walk up to strangers at church and recite long passages of Scripture to them or give them a revelatory word. We attended a very large church, and frequently people would seek us out, ask if this young child was ours, and then tell us how the Lord had spoken to them through him. It was a wonderful demonstration of the awe of God, and we were just as impacted as they were.

Even though Zachary was our first, we knew enough about children to realize that this was not typical four-year-old behavior. Nevertheless, while we recognized his gifting, we didn't lose sight of the fact that he was still just a child.

You may have a child who is "different." Our child was different — a cultural designation most children try very hard *not* to have. As parents, we aren't always comfortable with the description, either, and if we're not careful, we may start encouraging our children to do what they can to fit in, which, of course, is dangerously close to telling them to hide their giftings, or at least regulate them to certain times and places only.

If we start down this road, our children will be able to sense our discomfort — they're revelatory gifted, so, of course, they'll be able to discern that something isn't as it should be, and confusion will result. Their gifts come naturally to them, and if we are reluctant, even slightly, to accept what God has enabled them to do, they may begin to think that we are reluctant to accept them.

If we discourage our children's gifts, it is like trying to convince a girl who is tall for her age that she is actually average height or even short. The first day she goes to school, it will immediately become obvious to her that you are mistaken. She is then forced to draw one of several conclusions:

I am the tallest person in my grade, but my parents say I am short for my age. Therefore:

(1) my parents are not smart (as in, they cannot see the obvious);
(2) my parents are not honest with me (perhaps they are ashamed of the difference); or
(3) my parents are mistaken in this very obvious thing, so however much I love them, I probably cannot trust what they tell me.

Periodically, every child is apt to feel that he or she is "different" in one way or another, and our revelatory-gifted children may reach this conclusion much more frequently. Instead of playing down their differences, we should keep things out in the open and be honest and forthright:

"Yes, you are a ten-year-old who is taller than average. Some years you may be the tallest student in your grade, and some years someone else may be the tallest. In other words, you are very much like other children your age, but in some ways you are unique."

Our revelatory-gifted children need to know — from us — that yes, they have unique gifts but in most ways, they are very much like other children. Even the most gifted people have many more things in common with others than they have differences. All children can have supernatural experiences; it's just that some have them prolifically. All children have dreams, but some children are gifted and prolific dreamers. All children need a place where they can belong; they need a home that is their castle, where they are loved and can express love, where they are nurtured and raised in the love and admonition of the Lord.

Because differences sometimes war with their self-views, we need to be particularly mindful of helping our gifted children to be comfortable with themselves and their differences. Recognize that those differences can create potential difficulties but simultaneously open up possibilities for them as well. This is yet another reason we should never stop looking at our children as whole children, whose relationships, sense of identity, visions, and beliefs, as well as gifts, all need our attention.

Though gifted children have the same essential needs as other children, they have additional needs as well. Their gifts will impact virtually every facet of their lives: how they relate to people, how they play games (it's like playing cards with someone who knows what the other players are holding), how they do their schoolwork, how they mature in their emotions, and potentially more. All these are impacted by their gifts. If we gloss over their uniqueness, they will grow up without having their gifts nurtured, at the very least. But more likely, and more damaging, they will grow up with distrust and suspicion of adults in general — and probably with us in particular. They are also likely to conclude that we think something is wrong with them.

On the other end of the spectrum, if we overemphasize their abilities, they may become fearful of them, which would effectively shut down their "receivers" or close their spiritual eyes. Gifts that have been shut down typically require a good deal of time and patience to reopen.

Another negative result of focusing too much on the gift is that it trains our children to do the same. They will be inclined to compare themselves constantly with other children, trying to determine whether they are more or less gifted than their friends and whether or not their gifts make them good or bad. A better perspective is that everyone is unique, and it is our differences that make life so interesting and demonstrate how awesome God is. We should convey to our children that each of us needs to become the person that God created us to be, whatever that looks like.

Revelatory-gifted Children and Destiny

As we've briefly mentioned, parents sometimes make the mistake of assuming that if their children are revelatory in some way, it must mean that they're called to full-time ministry. This isn't always the case. In fact, we'd venture to say that it is rarely the case. Revelatory-gifted children may feel called to be pianists or ball players, janitors or doctors. Our children are imbued with many attributes in addition to revelatory gifting, and as parents we need to nurture all of those gifts.

We set the stage for our children. Proverbs 22:6 instructs us to train them in the way they should go. This speaks of training them in the knowledge of God, yes, but it also means that we should train them in the way that each of them individually is supposed to go. We shouldn't expect to find peaches on a hickory tree, and we shouldn't try to fashion weight lifters from ballet dancers — in other words, we shouldn't try to direct our revelatory-gifted children into full-time ministry if they feel called to business, medicine, teaching, or some other occupation.

Like all children, spiritually gifted children need to develop their incredible potential. Raised in the right environment, they will have the same interest, drive, curiosity, and fortitude about their giftings that athletically, musically, and otherwise gifted children express. In that, however, we face some difficulty. If our children have athletic gifting, we know what would help develop that gifting. All we need to do is find an athletic team or other sports venue in which they can participate. Finding music teachers or dance instructors isn't all that challenging, either. But how are we supposed to help them grow in their revelatory giftings? It is not quite as obvious what groups, venues, and environments will serve that purpose. If we aren't revelatory gifted ourselves, how are we supposed to raise children who are? It can still be difficult even if we are so gifted.

As we seek to answer the questions above, one element remains the same: the need for good character, integrity, and courage. If our children's character is strong and they are seeking to build intimacy with God, their gifts will naturally grow and develop as well.

There are, however, some key steps we can take in order to nurture our children in this area. In addition to helping them further develop their giftings through spiritual exercises (please see the appendix at the end of the book), we need to validate their revelations and help them develop their decision-making ability.

Validating Revelations
As parents, one of the most important things we could do for our children is validate them in what God is telling them. They need us to acknowledge that they are hearing from God, seeing real angels, having real experiences — and that these things matter.

A few summers ago, we were in England with our two daughters. Greg and Sarah were driving on to Scotland, while Anna and I were flying to Ireland.

At dinner the night before our friends left with Greg and Sarah, they asked me how we were getting to Ireland. I explained that I had planned to take the tube (London's subway) to the Liverpool Street Station and then the train to Stansted Airport; from there we would fly to Shannon. Our friends agreed that was the best way to go. After everyone left, Annie and I took the tube back to our hotel.

We had a great walk through the South Kensington area of London, with all its bustle and activity even late in the evening. We talked about where we had been and speculated about Ireland and what it might be like, as neither of us had ever been there. As we got to the hotel, I had a spontaneous thought. I turned to Anna and told her that rather than take the tube in the morning, I thought we should take a taxi. She quickly agreed, and I ordered the taxi from the desk as we went by.

This was not my natural inclination for a number of reasons. For one thing, a taxi normally takes longer than the underground tube during rush hour. Also, they cost much more than the tube. Combine that with the unfavorable exchange rate for the dollar to the pound sterling — and me on a ministry budget — it didn't make very much sense why I would change our plans like that. But it felt like the right thing to do.

In the morning, the taxi was waiting for us, and we

headed to Liverpool Street Station to catch the train. Amazingly, on this morning the taxi was quite expedient, and we reached the train station a little ahead of our schedule. We boarded the train for the airport without incident. However, the moment we reached the airport, we noticed that something seemed amiss. We dismissed it at first, but after a while, the sense that something was wrong grew more and more obvious. All the passengers for our flight were cordoned off to a particular area to wait for the plane. Airport personnel kept paging a certain passenger from an earlier flight, saying that if the passenger didn't show up immediately, the plane would be deboarded, baggage removed, and the passenger wouldn't be allowed to travel that day.

When we landed and disembarked from our short flight to Ireland, the televisions in the terminal displayed scene after scene of bombings in London. Passengers on the tube near the Liverpool Street Station were among the victims. Anna and I stood there in shock. My daughter started crying.

"Mom, that is where we were," she said.

If we had followed our original plan, we likely would have seen the bombings firsthand underground.

"I knew we weren't supposed to take the tube!" Anna said.

In the midst of my shock, revulsion, anxiety, and adrenalin, an old habit surfaced. "That's right, Annie," I told her. "You were hearing from God. That was the Holy Spirit speaking to you, training you to hear God's voice."

Wherever we are is a good place to nurture our revelatory-gifted children. It requires only that we pay attention and communicate. When we go out of our way to give importance to them and what God has revealed to them, our children will be even more interested in communicating with Him next time.

Developing Decision-making Ability
Revelatory-gifted children face certain challenges that other children may not have to face. One of these challenges is learn-

ing how to make decisions that are based on wisdom and common sense and not just on revelation. In some situations, revelation can give our children "a leg up," so to speak, but it also can create quandaries.

A very gifted friend of ours once said that while in school, he hadn't studied; he had just prayed for revelation. That was all he needed to do, and he passed his exams. We didn't find this story particularly helpful. Revelatory children can learn early on how to rely on their giftings to accomplish what others do with study and discipline. This is not always a blessing. The skills children cultivate in school — discipline, planning, knowing how to learn and process, etc. — are valuable for life, and all of our children need to master them. When our children make decisions based on revelation, it isn't truly decision making; it is responding to revelation — something that ebbs and flows. If they don't know how to make sound decisions on their own, what will they do when the revelation is momentarily absent?

Let's say a sixteen-year-old has just received her driver's license, and she wants to go across town to visit a friend. She has been to her friend's house only a few times before but knows she can get there with a combination of memory and revelation. She is very sensitive to the Spirit, so she probably could do this without any trouble. However, what if she gets to the center of town, and today is a day when her revelatory gifting is ebbing? Does she know how to read a map?

Raising revelatory children includes helping them differentiate between revelatory and cognitive thought processes. These two elements don't oppose each other; when both are developed, each enhances the other.

In addition, based on the revelation God has given them, can they actually make the best choice? Just because they know something doesn't mean they should act on what they know.

For example, Joey asks Sam to come and play tomorrow afternoon, but after he does, Billy asks Sam — in front of Joey — to go to the movies with him tomorrow. Sam likes to play with both boys, and he knows that if he doesn't accept Billy's offer now, Billy will just invite someone else to go to the movies with him.

Here's the problem: Through his gifting, Sam knows that something is going to come up for Joey's Mom that will cancel tomorrow's play date. While it might seem expedient to go ahead and cancel on Joey, knowing he won't be able to play anyway, that would hurt Joey's feelings. Joey doesn't have the revelation Sam has, and Sam knows that Joey would feel rejected. So what is he to do?

Through this little story, you can see how this sort of revelatory information doesn't help Sam make a decision; in fact, it makes the process worse. We should never underestimate the difficulties that our revelatory children have with simple day-to-day things. Revelation doesn't always make things simpler.

In another example, ten-year-old Dave was invited by a well-known prophetic minister to go to a leaders' meeting. Dave liked this minister. He was a family friend, and Dave was happy to go with him. Afterward, when his mom asked him if he'd had a good time, Dave replied, "It was okay, but Pastor Jones didn't want me there."

Pastor Jones was one of the local ministers and a leader in the community. Trying to help (and to deal with anyone who might not have been nice to her child), his mother asked, "What did Pastor Jones say?"

"Oh, he acted very friendly," Dave said. "He told me, 'How nice that you could come,' but he was actually thinking, *Why did he bring Dave? Dave doesn't belong here, and I don't want him here. My own kids should be here before Dave is.*"

Based on the vocabulary and manner of speech, it was clear to Sam's mom that he was probably accurately reporting Pastor Jones' thoughts. His mom also knew that this was an important moment for Dave and that she had to respond wisely.

When our children pick up on another person's anger or annoyance — which they all will at some point — we don't want to deny the truth by suggesting the person didn't really mean that. If we do, we're making a poor experience worse. Instead, we want to encourage our children to do two things: One, they should recognize that yes, they have truly discerned the person's feelings; and two, they shouldn't do anything that would provoke the person. A clever child can easily set up another person to reveal his or her soulishness (personal short-comings) and therefore look foolish.

If our children can recognize that a person's soulishness is that person's problem, they can learn to accept it as such and not receive it as rejection. They can then make a decision based on the merits of the situation and not on the other person's emotional response.

Revelatory people (adults and children alike) can be highly susceptible to rejection. It would be very easy for Dave to start thinking, *Why wouldn't he want me there? Something must be wrong with me. Maybe everybody there disliked me.* We don't want to put someone who is operating at a soul level in a place of influence in our children's lives.

Dave's mother responded well. She didn't deny that he had perceived Pastor Jones' thoughts correctly. Instead, she pointed out that it was too bad Pastor Jones felt that way and suggested they pray for him. Perhaps the Lord would heal whatever it was that had made him feel like that.

By responding this way, she validated her child's perceptions and removed the negativity. Dave didn't take on any harmful thoughts about himself and responded the way God intended. Eventually, Pastor Jones fell into ill repute and lost his church position and a good deal more, but Dave didn't have to worry that he had harbored any ill will toward the man, because he had prayed for him and for God's will in his life.

Simply put, our revelatory-gifted children need to learn that in some cases they can make decisions based on revelation, but sometimes they need to make decisions in spite of revelation.

In Conclusion

Revelation is not solely for a special group of children and adults who are somehow "more holy" than the rest. Everyone has the ability to communicate with God, whether we were raised in a Christian home or not.

What is the most important thing we could understand about revelation? That it isn't about revelation — it's about relationship with the Father. In a moment of great revelation, Jeremiah (9:24) was told by God, "'Let him who boasts boast of this, that he understands and knows Me, that I am the LORD."

This is the most important thing we need to learn about revelatory gifting: Everyone, Christians and non-Christians alike, can have dreams or prophetic words, but in order to understand correctly what God is saying to us, relationship with Him is key. It is vital that we help our children grasp this fact. We need to know Him, know about Him, and understand His ways.

Something to Ponder

Just say "Oh"

Several years ago, Greg was on staff at a church filled with young couples. They believed in having children. I cannot count the times some young mom with five children under the age of six and a monthly household income of two thousand dollars, for example, would announce that she was pregnant.

Looking at it in the natural, some of us would quickly conclude, *This isn't good news at all, on any number of fronts.* Some of those women felt the same. They were already overwhelmed and exhausted, and they floundered at the thought of being pregnant yet again. However, many of these young families were thrilled, and they didn't seem concerned at the thought of potential difficulties.

I (Patricia) couldn't always tell if the mother wanted congratulations or encouragement, so I learned to say, "Ohhhh." By drawing out that one-syllable response, I gave my spirit time to pray: *Oh, God! Oh, God! What should I say? How should I respond?*

These parents didn't need my opinion about their lives; they needed someone to share their burden, if it was a burden, and their joy, if it was a joy. Often, of course, it was both, and God knew exactly what they needed to hear in the moment, all my "expertise" aside.

Greg and I have found that one of the most important things we could do for our children is to not have all the answers. In fact, many times, having the answer can be a hindrance. Instead, we should take a quiet moment to pray before responding, because this helps us to listen. Remember that we are not raising our children to look to us but to God.

When your children come running up to tell you something, first of all, be mindful of the glib response. Even if the story sounds incredibly bizarre or you're certain they made up the dream, experience, or angelic encounter, still take a moment to say, "Ohhhh," and then listen to them and listen to God. Be led by the Spirit.

Along with this, perhaps there are times you just *know* the interpretation of one of their dreams. Even here, take a moment to say, "Ohhhh," and let God speak to their hearts about it. Does your interpretation have an expiration date of right now? Probably not.

We are nurturing our children toward God, not ourselves. Even though we as their parents are providing for them in tangible ways, our desire is for them to find God as their Source. Every dream is an opportunity to explore and advance in communication with God and in the understanding of His ways.

When the occasion arises, and you're faced with an unknown or have an opportunity to speak into your children's lives, what should you do?

1. Stop yourself. Pause. Take a moment to say, "Ohhhh," or whatever works for you.

2. Listen to both your children and to God. Where is God wanting to lead your children? What do your children think about it?

3. Ask a few questions: "What are you thinking? What does it feel like? Have you considered . . . ?"

If your children can listen to God and come to a good understanding and interpretation based on what He's told them — that is the best. If they need more input from you, that is good, too, but keep the process as the most important thing. The process is what leads them to communion with their God.

Chapter 8

Nurturing Your Children's Giftings

In a previous chapter, we talked about how our children are special just for who they are, not because they are spiritual or gifted. This distinction is important in order for them to learn to put God first in their lives. If they think they are special because they are gifted, the gifting and its success will be their focus. They won't be willing to do anything that would potentially allow them to fail, because failure, in their minds, would be a deathblow to who they are.

Unfortunately, it is a very easy thing for parents to blur the lines between the specialness of the giftings and the specialness of the children. When our children show an aptitude for something, be it revelation, mathematics, or anything else, it delights us, and we show them that delight. But we need to make certain we are just as delighted in their personality and character as we are in their giftings, or else they will learn that their giftings are the most important thing about them.

Mary, the mother of Jesus, is an excellent example of navigating this territory. Obviously she knew how special her Son was, but she didn't try to exalt Him.

When Jesus was about twelve, His mother and father lost track of Him on their way home from Jerusalem. We all know the story:

> So when they did not find Him, they returned to Jerusalem, seeking Him. Now so it was that after three days they found Him in the temple, sitting in

> *the midst of the teachers, both listening to them and asking them questions. And all who heard Him were astonished at His understanding and answers. So when they saw Him, they were amazed; and His mother said to Him, "Son, why have You done this to us? Look, Your father and I have sought You anxiously."*
>
> *And He said to them, "Why did you seek Me? Did you not know that I must be about My Father's business?" But they did not understand the statement which He spoke to them.*
> — Luke 2:45–50, NKJV

This verse is what we need to see:

> *Then He went down with them and came to Nazareth, and was subject to them, but His mother kept all these things in her heart.* **And Jesus increased in wisdom and stature, and in favor with God and men.**
> — Luke 2:51–52, NKJV, *emphasis ours*

Destiny has a way of making room for itself, which means that if our child is the next Moses, Beethoven, or Thomas Edison, we don't need to tell anyone. When our children come into their destinies, people will know. In the meantime, we can all learn a great lesson from Mary, who knew of the greatness of her Child but didn't strive to make that greatness known. No doubt as Jesus grew up, He daily demonstrated just how incredible and awesome He truly is. But Mary didn't go out and call attention to Him. She didn't organize meetings to demonstrate what a unique and gifted person He is or try to convince the religious leaders that she had what they needed. Mary didn't take any of these actions. Instead, Scripture says that she kept all these things in her heart. In other words, she kept them to herself:

*After seeing Him, the shepherds told everyone what
had happened and what the angel had said to them
about this child. All who heard the shepherds' story
were astonished, but Mary kept all these things in
her heart and thought about them often.*
— Luke 2:17–19

Jesus was subject to His parents, and they raised Him in such a way that He grew in wisdom and stature, as well as in favor with God and man. Even though both His parents knew He was the Son of God, molding His character was on the top of their list.

Luke 2:19 is the ultimate guide for how we are to raise our children and nurture their giftings. Mary knew what Jesus was capable of (John 2:5), and yet she also knew that her role in His life was to be His mother. To teach Him and train Him. To care for Him and protect Him. Her role wasn't to tell people who He was going to be, how gifted He was, or how much they needed to give Him glory. She hadn't facilitated those meetings with the elders, and in fact, she was upset when they occurred!

*"Son," his mother said to him, "why have you done
this to us? Your father and I have been frantic,
searching for you everywhere."*
— Luke 2:48

In most cases, Scripture requires meditation and study in order for us to understand what it is saying in depth, but in this case we believe it to be clear and succinct. Mothers and fathers, this is our road map for child rearing — we need to do it in such a way that our children learn what Jesus learned: wisdom and stature (character), which in turn will give them favor with God and humanity.

We don't need to promote them. Obviously, this doesn't mean that we should hide them away or deny their giftings; nor does it mean that we shouldn't invite relatives and friends to their piano recitals or science fairs. It simply means that our responsibility is to raise them, not to direct the spotlight. We aren't nurturing celebrities who need a following; we are creating whole and healthy sons and daughters of God who are capable of using their gifts in a manner that expresses His love and hope.

Greg and I have witnessed the painful, long-lasting aftereffects of parents who have forced their children into the limelight. Many years ago we belonged to a church that was the recipient of a sudden, intense move of God. The Holy Spirit began to pour Himself out on the children in the school, and they were having all manner of spiritual experiences. There were healings, angelic visitations, and more; lives were being transformed.

But only weeks later, the move of God stopped as suddenly as it had begun. After it had been promoted, told abroad, and shown off to the world, it was over, just that fast. Many church and school members were devastated — not necessarily because the move had ended but because of what had happened before it ended.

When we think back to that experience, we can see two major factors that seemed to be involved in the move's cessation. First, what started as something the Holy Sprit was doing in the children became something owned by the parents. Many of them — certainly not all, but many — wanted to be sure that their children were showcased. They seemed to feel that what happened to the children glorified the parents, and they responded accordingly.

Great problems occur whenever the created think they can own what the Creator is doing. The purpose of the revelatory gifts is for the work of ministry and to demonstrate who God is — His attributes, personality, glory, and love. We must not try to take His glory, even a little bit, for ourselves.

Second, some of the parents wanted the move to be about holiness. Certain children were deemed not holy enough to participate, even though some of them had been having amazing encounters and evidenced the most profound revelations. These externally "unholy children" were subtly kept back, and the externally "holy children" were promoted. What an example of how we lose sight of the spiritual and replace it with religiousness!

Decades have passed, but what happened is still a controversy and a source of upset for many, many people, some of whom carry regret, guilt, anger, and a host of other emotions — not at God but at the conduct of adults and the fallout for the children. Sadly, the situation estranged some of those children from God (and more of them from the Church), because He was interpreted in a hurtful way, one that did not sanctify His nature or accurately model who He is.

One of those children we will call Abby. Recently, she and several Christian leaders attended a meeting. Someone had asked for prayer, and Burt, a man who had been a spiritual father to these kids back in the day, asked Abby to pray.

Instead, she began to weep. When she was finally able to pray, she had a revelation that led to the healing of the woman who had come for prayer.

Afterward, Burt asked Abby what was the matter. For years, she had borne an incredible amount of guilt, thinking that she was responsible for ending the move of God when she was a child. Why did she feel this way? Because that was what she and the other children had been told! It had been communicated to them, both openly and by inference, that the Holy Spirit had lifted because some of the children weren't holy enough and weren't spending enough time in prayer. Condemnation had consumed years of her life.

Again, not all the children were so negatively affected; some of these young adults light up as they recount their experiences during that season. But many others have been left to flounder with guilt and rejection because adults either couldn't or wouldn't take responsibility for their own actions. It was a time unlike any other of our lives, and almost twenty years later, many of us wish there could be a "do over."

This can be one result of focusing on the gifting more than the child. Gifting speaks for itself. We do not have to speak for it.

Are we suggesting that you avoid speaking well of your children and encouraging them in their gifts? No. Should you be cautious about asking God to bless them? Again, no. You just need to be aware of your role as a parent, and then walk forward in authority and humility. Create an incubator for your children: a nurturing environment in which they can learn about God, grow closer to Him, and explore their giftings.

In Conclusion

Great artistry, musicianship, and talent are incredible. Dreams, visions, signs, and wonders are exciting — and we have the promise of even greater things to come (John 14:12). But our most important role is cultivating our children's character. We need to keep our focus on who our children are becoming and not on their gifts.

Our job is not to become our children's public relations specialists. However excited we may be about what God is doing with and for them, we should let them set the tempo for how much to share with other people. We then should honor their boundaries.

Remember, just like Mary, we are raising our children to "go out." With adulthood comes the passing of the baton, and we must make today count so that when it comes time to let go, we are satisfied that we did all we could.

Another important point to remember comes from 1 Corinthians 15:46: "What comes first is the natural body, then the spiritual body comes later." Jesus was God at birth; He did not become God — He was already God. But He worked no public miracles in His childhood. Though He confounded the scholars when He was twelve, He "was subject" to His parents (Luke 2:51, NKJV), and "grew in wisdom and in stature and in favor with God and all the people" (Luke 2:52).

Jesus worked no public miracles until He was thirty.

What was He doing all that time? Was He somehow wasting His God-given gifting? No, He was becoming wholesomely and fully human ("natural") before becoming fully spiritual. Our spiritually gifted children need their childhood in order to become balanced, human, and wholesome in character; they need to be children before becoming or being asked to be spiritually mature.

First the natural, then the spiritual. A great tragedy is that many children have been developed into spiritual giants but have never learned how to be wholesomely human, as Jesus was and is.

Something to Ponder

What's "Missing" in Your Life?

It is a conundrum in our lives that when we sense something is missing, we focus on what is wrong instead of what is going well.

Greg and I would suggest that some of the things you feel are missing from your life are actually present, but the cares of life, the rush of schedules, and "problems" may have captured all of your attention. If that is true, then at least part of your solution is to put your attention on new things.

Instead of focusing on the void, focus on and search out what is in your life that you are currently not seeing.

1. Write down three things that you would like to have in your life: time to read, healthy meals, playing board games, quiet time, exercise, engaging your spouse on interests (more than child or financial issues), etc.

2. Take out your calendar and plan (both date and time) to do each of these things at least once a week for the next month. Make the appointment just as firmly as you would a doctor's appointment or business meeting, and then keep it.

3. Be on the lookout for those small, special times that will be just what you are looking for.

4. Be disciplined to focus your attention on what you are doing, what you have in your life, and not on the things that are wrong

or missing. Problems need to be solved and issues need to be addressed, but those are different than dwelling or focusing on what is wrong or missing in your life.

Remember, we get what we put our attention on. What we search for, we will find. That is the principle of Philippians 4:6–8:

> *Don't worry about anything; instead, pray about everything. Tell God what you need, and thank Him for all He has done. Then you will experience God's peace, which exceeds anything we can understand. His peace will guard your hearts and minds as you live in Christ Jesus.*

> *And now, dear brothers and sisters, one final thing. Fix your thoughts on what is true, and honorable, and right, and pure, and lovely, and admirable. Think about things that are excellent and worthy of praise.*

Chapter 9

Understanding Children's Dreams

For God may speak in one way, or in another,
Yet man does not perceive it.

In a dream, in a vision of the night,
When deep sleep falls upon men,
While slumbering on their beds,

Then He opens the ears of men,
And seals their instruction.

In order to turn man from his deed,
And conceal pride from man,
— Job 33:14–17, NKJV

It was a typical morning at our house. As a pastor's wife with four children for breakfast, lunch, and dinner, plus homeschooling and whatever else was on the schedule that day, it was sometimes a challenge to keep the ship moving forward in any semblance of order.

This particular morning, things were going along swimmingly until little Sarah bounced into the kitchen. She was as aggravated as a five-year-old could be.

Considering everything else that was going on that morning, I wasn't all that focused on nurturing her gifting, but I did know Sarah, and it was clear to me that the best way to execute my agenda was to take a few minutes to resolve whatever had upset her.

"I had a dream," she firmly declared. "A tornado was coming right down Brown Avenue, and it was ruining everything."

It had never occurred to me that Sarah felt so strongly about the condition of Brown Avenue on the whole, but it wasn't hard to see that she didn't approve of a tornado making matchsticks of her house! I really wanted to get breakfast over with, so I told her, "Well, let's pray that no tornado comes down Brown Avenue."

We prayed, and afterward everyone seemed satisfied. At least Sarah was. So we went on with breakfast, and the matter was mostly forgotten.

Two weeks later, Greg and I were at the church for a training session with our home group leaders. The phone began to ring in the office. We were a little annoyed that someone would call in the middle of a meeting — obviously, if they knew we were there, they knew we were in a meeting. The annoyance was quickly dismissed, however, when the caller very anxiously reported that sirens were going off all over town, and there were several tornadoes touching down. We hustled everyone out of the church, ran to our van, and raced toward Brown Avenue and our four children at home.

We pulled onto the main thoroughfare and headed westbound, one mile north of the freeway. I turned on the radio, and the report said that the tornado was headed eastbound, one mile north of the freeway. It was approaching the major cross street near our house. I let out a moderate scream, but Greg focused on reaching the house.

When we arrived, the television was on, and the children were huddled in the hallway. The report continued to say that the tornado was headed eastbound on the north side of the freeway — right for us. It was then I remembered Sarah's dream and our prayer.

That stormy night, the tornado did not touch down on

Brown Avenue, which was directly in its path. Instead, it touched down on the south side of the freeway — out of its projected path. Our house, our neighbor's houses, and Brown Avenue in its entirety were spared. The tornado didn't harm any homes and took out only some storage buildings. Though most people probably didn't realize how much they had been spared that night, one five-year-old girl got the lesson of a lifetime: Dreams can be from God, revelation is real, and God answers prayer.

First Samuel 1 contains the well-known story of Hannah and her firstborn, the little boy Samuel who heard God's voice. Hannah had been barren for years, but then God answered her prayers and gave her a son. In keeping with the promise she had made to God, once the boy was old enough, she entrusted him to Eli the priest.

One night as Samuel slept, the Lord came to speak with him:

Samuel was sleeping in the Tabernacle near the Ark of God. Suddenly the Lord called out, "Samuel!"

"Yes?" Samuel replied. "What is it?" He got up and ran to Eli. "Here I am. Did you call me?"

"I didn't call you," Eli replied. "Go back to bed." So he did.

Then the Lord called out again, "Samuel!"

Again Samuel got up and went to Eli. "Here I am. Did you call me?"

"I didn't call you, my son," Eli said. "Go back to bed."

Samuel did not yet know the Lord because he had never had a message from the Lord before. So the Lord called a third time, and once more Samuel got up and went to Eli. "Here I am. Did you call me?"

Then Eli realized it was the Lord who was calling the boy. So he said to Samuel, "Go and lie down again, and if someone calls again, say, 'Speak, Lord, your servant is listening.'" So Samuel went back to bed.

And the Lord came and called as before, "Samuel! Samuel!"

And Samuel replied, "Speak, your servant is listening."
— 1 Samuel 3:3–10

Like many of us, Eli had his failings (specifically, he had failed in raising his own sons), but in spite of those failings, he was able to raise Samuel to become a great man who had a firm understanding of God and His ways. He gave the boy good guidance. Samuel became a leader of the nation of Israel, and today he is one of the greatest examples we have of what a fruitful revelatory person looks like.

Where Do Dreams Come From?

As we seek to guide our children in the realm of revelation, dreams, and visions, we will often feel as though we are in over our heads. Perhaps we will even feel lost and not have a clue what to do next. But our children don't need all the answers and expertise at every turn. They just need our love and good basic direction.

In order to help our children comprehend their dreams, we first need to understand where different dreams come from.

Have you ever heard someone refer to a dream as a "pizza dream"? It isn't rare to have dreams that are physiological in origin — that is, birthed from physical sources such as what we ate or the late hour we went to bed. Dreams can also be psychological in that they are our human means of processing the input and emotions in our lives. Some dreams cause us to relive experiences and conversations and force us to face our fears; in dreams we may be able to answer questions better, understand what we didn't understand before, or release the energy from an emotionally charged relationship or experience.

However, not all dreams are physiological or psychological in nature. Some of them, such as Sarah's dream about the tornado, are clearly more than that. When we are asleep, our bodies, minds, wills, and emotions are in a state of suspension; our spirits are not. Even though our bodies sleep, our spirits are awake, and in this position, we are actually much more open to hearing God's voice, particularly about matters that we might ignore while awake.

For instance, if we have decided that we will *never* live somewhere with snow, a word about moving to northern Canada might not even register on our spirit's "radar," because the radar is already set to eliminate such words. *That couldn't be God*, we immediately think and then move on. Knowing this, God might broach the subject while we're asleep, thereby side-stepping our objections.

Dreams can be answers to prayer, encouragement, preparation for future events, times of healing, and more — all of them given to us while we're not conscious enough to argue them away. They can be times of communion with God.

Finally, dreams can also come from the enemy. These typically fall into the categories of nightmares and spiritual warfare dreams, both of which we will be discussing in greater detail.

We often hear people ask if children have more dreams than adults. We don't think that's the case. We do believe, however, that children are more aware of their dreams. This may be because most of us learn while growing up that dreams are not important and therefore they should be given little value. Telling our children it was "only a dream" is one of the most damaging things parents can do to their children's spirituality. What would have happened if Eli had told young Samuel, "It was just a dream"? What would have happened if Sarah's tornado dream had been dismissed instead of prayed about?

We won't always have the answers, an explanation, or the exact interpretation for our children, but we can always take a moment to pray with them about the dream and acknowledge that they are hearing from God.

In addition to the symbols and methods for interpreting dreams included in this chapter, we also include a list of resources in the back of this book if you would like to do more study on this topic.

Metaphors in Dreams

> *"Hear now My words:*
> *If there is a prophet among you,*
> *I, the LORD, make Myself known to him in a vision;*
> *I speak to him in a dream.*
>
> *Not so with My servant Moses;*
> *He is faithful in all My house.*
>
> *I speak with him face to face,*
> *Even plainly, and not in dark sayings;*
> *And he sees the form of the LORD.*
> *Why then were you not afraid*
> *To speak against My servant Moses?"*
> — Numbers 12:6–8, NKJV

God had a special relationship with Moses. He spoke to him directly — plainly, clearly, face to face — but to everyone else, He spoke in "dark sayings." *Dark* here doesn't mean something inherently negative; it means something that isn't overtly clear. To help explain this further, the New Living Translation refers to God's communications in the previous passage as "riddles," something that we need to search out in order to understand. That *searching out* is the key.

Revelation is an invitation. Whenever God gives us dreams or otherwise communicates something we don't understand, He is inviting us into deeper intimacy and a secret life with Him. As Proverbs 25:2 says, God conceals things so that kings will search them out and discover them: He is seeking relationship with us. We respond to God by searching Him out, dwelling on His secrets, uncovering His hidden meanings, and pursuing Him and His mystery. The Bible highlights the importance of spending time with Him and meditating on Him not only with its content but also with the words themselves.

Ancient Hebrew, the original language of God's chosen people, was a pictographic language, much like Egyptian hieroglyphics; each word was formed with a series of pictures. They were "riddles" — word pictures (metaphors) that needed to be translated.

Dreams reflect the metaphorical way He communicates. Some, like Sarah's dream of the tornado, are prophetic calls to intercession. Some are literal, but most are stories that need interpretation. We can think of them as *pictures* of what God is saying.

For example, if God wants to show Tiffany His love, she could dream about her dad (the Father) coming and giving her a hug. That would be a somewhat simple dream to interpret. If God wants Matt to know that He's about to bring him favor in his area of gifting, Matt could dream about standing in front of a group of people and doing what he's gifted to do. God will speak to us in accordance with our age and understanding, so children's dreams and spiritual experiences are often simpler than the dreams and spiritual experiences of adults.

How do we begin to understand what God is saying in our children's dreams? First, we need to be dependent on the Holy Spirit's revelation. Only through His help will we correctly understand the dreams He gives us. Second, we need to build our understanding of what metaphors commonly mean.

Some metaphors are biblical in nature. When these appear in dreams, they often mean what they mean in the Bible: Seeds represent the Word of God (Matthew 13:19), hair can mean glory (1 Corinthians 11:15), cows can mean provision (Genesis 41:25–27), etc.

When a dream element isn't in the Bible (such as a soccer game or a minivan), a general understanding of idioms and common sense may help us reach greater understanding. For example, cats are naturally very independent, graceful creatures, so they often represent strategic thinking or something that is slinking and treacherous.

We should expect homonyms in dreams (a pear could symbolize a pair) and other wordplays. But, once again, we need to maintain a strong dependency on the Holy Spirit's guidance. Symbolism is two-fold: Most symbols have a positive and negative meaning. A good example of this, bees are often thought to represent the demonic, but they also can represent industry and provision. "God uses double meanings for most symbols to keep us from jumping to conclusions and so that we will ponder, pray, and ask," John Loren Sandford says. In other words, God does this so that we will search Him out. Only then will we discover the meaning.

This being the case, some dreams aren't fully understood for years. There is also the issue of interruption. When children realize they are having an important dream, sometimes they wake themselves up before the dream is completed. At other times, they can be so excited to have heard Him that they don't wait for Him to finish. God wants to give them a foot-long revelation, but they take off after seeing the first two inches. If they share a dream with us, and we don't understand what it means, this could be one reason.

Dreams also have different levels of meaning. We may feel that we know what a dream means today, but five years from now, we'll realize it meant a good deal more. In that case, the first interpretation wasn't wrong; it was merely one "layer" of the dream. Dreams such as this tend to stay with our children and occupy a back corner of their thoughts. The day they come to pass, our children are amazed at how God orchestrated their circumstances.

Also, we need to keep in mind that dreams aren't always clear-cut and perfectly defined. Even if we have a basic understanding of what a dream means, we may not have all the details. Let's say that Johnny dreams about his friend Tim breaking his leg, but the dream doesn't reveal how or when; Johnny just knows that it's going to happen. We can trust God to give our children better understanding when and if they need it.

In summation, to help our children understand what God is saying in their dreams, we need a basic comprehension of common metaphors and a strong dependency on the Holy Spirit, who is more than willing to explain anything we need to have explained. Dream interpretation is an issue of practice, one that most of us will be able to grow in.

Personal Metaphors

Adults and children alike have their own dream languages — certain elements that mean certain things to them personally based on their interests and past experiences. It is possible for one person's dream language to be similar to another person's, but each will also have distinct differences.

For example, most Christian symbol resources will tell you that in some dreams dogs can be evil, and Dora would agree. She is terribly afraid of dogs. If she dreams about a big black dog chasing her, it would be scary to her and would no doubt represent something dark.

However, large black dogs would not mean the same for us. Our family had a huge, black, scary-looking dog who was just a big puppy at heart. We loved him, and he loved us. So if someone in our family dreams about a big black dog, it may represent a faithful friend, not a threat.

It is good for us to understand and memorize biblical symbols and common metaphors, and we also want to help our children cultivate their own dream language. We'll be talking more about the importance of journaling at the end of this chapter, but one of its benefits is that over time, we will be able to see patterns and repetition in our children's dreams, which will help us identify elements in their personal dream language.

Most dreamers begin to recognize that certain individuals represent to them specific virtues, occupations, or even the Lord in their dreams. For example, Greg is a person who carries a lot of natural and spiritual authority. Countless people have told us that they have had dreams with Greg in them, and in their dreams they believe that he often represents authority. This happens with people in church, people who work for him in both secular and ministry settings, and even people he doesn't know personally. Whenever a certain authority figure keeps reappearing in our children's dreams, he or she could be representing God — or His authority at least.

We should keep in mind that, like children, our personal dream language will grow over time, and metaphors may adjust or evolve to mean different things than they have meant in the past.

Determining the Focus

When interpreting a dream, one of the first things we need to discern is the dream's focus. Is the dream about Billie? Or is the dream really about the neighbor, and Billie is just a participant or observer in the dream? An easy test is this: If we were to take Billie out of the dream, does the dream change at all? If not, then Billie isn't the focus.

If your children have a hard time comprehending what focus means, you can help them by talking about their favorite picture books. Stories often have a narrator or a main character. In a dream, when the child is the "narrator," the focus or main character is someone else. But when the child is acting and participating in the dream, he or she is the main character and therefore the focus of the dream. Knowing the dream's focus is a key to understanding what it means.

Types of Children's Dreams

Below is a list of common children's dreams, what they typically mean, and what we as parents can do about them. We will be discussing nightmares and nightmare prevention in the next chapter.

Self-condition (or Environment) Dreams

One night, seven-year-old Brad dreamed that a snake was trying to eat him. His mother knew that snakes usually have a negative meaning and typically represent rebelliousness, cunning, and general opposition to God. The basic interpretation of the dream was that someone or something opposed to the things of God was also opposing Brad. His mother hadn't meant anything by the conversation, but afterward Brad was very quiet, and she asked him what was wrong.

He had recently started hanging out with a certain group of kids at school. He was flattered by their attention and intrigued at the idea of becoming more popular. But at the same time, he knew that joining the group probably wasn't a good idea. They often got in trouble and were already pressuring him to do and say things he knew weren't right. When he heard the meaning of his dream, Brad knew what God was asking him to do.

When situations like this occur, teach your children how to take authority in their lives by recognizing and being grateful for the warning, and then pray with them.

Six-year-old Bailey also dreamed that a snake was trying to eat her. The next day at school, she got in trouble for something she hadn't done. Libby, the class bully and the real culprit, had lied and told the teacher it was Bailey.

These are examples of self-condition or environment dreams. Many children's dreams fall into this category. They can be specifically about the children and their circumstances or about their surroundings: family, friends, school, neighborhood, church and school groups, and more. Not every dream in this category will require a lot of interpretation. When you're dependent on the Holy Spirit to guide you, your acquired knowledge of symbols and metaphors will enhance your understanding and comprehension.

If the meaning of the self-condition dream doesn't appear right away, we can potentially help it come to light by asking a few questions. "Were you scared? Was it going to hurt you? How did you feel?" Questions such as these may help reveal what God was saying.

Certain self-condition dreams we should accept with caution. As we stated in Chapter 7, our children will occasionally, or perhaps frequently, receive revelations about a person or issue, but this doesn't mean they should go to the person or tell others about it. In some cases, the information they have could be potentially embarrassing for the person involved. When considering any action, we need to be led by the Holy Spirit.

This remains true even when we feel we know exactly what the dream is telling our children to do. We can talk to them about it, help them consider their options, and develop a clear perspective of the situation, but we can't force them to follow through. That is between them and God.

One of the wonderful things about self-condition/environment dreams is that they enable our children to see first by the Holy Spirit (revelation) and then by the natural. What God is saying about the situation is always so much more important than what the situation itself seems to be saying.

Destiny Dreams

Children typically have a number of destiny (or calling) dreams over the course of their childhood, and each one may be about a different topic; the destiny itself may seem to jump back and forth between different occupations or ideas. Obviously, this isn't because God cannot decide what our children should do with their lives. We are multi-faceted people, and there are many components and attributes that we assimilate on the road to our destinies. Many of these components may be imparted to us in our dreams.

In destiny dreams God can also be showing our children what they *could* do. Not every destiny dream is a set-instone, this-is-your-life destiny dream. Some of them may be, but others are just highlighting options and potentials that God is making available to our children.

For instance, let's say a little boy dreams one night that he is a great preacher. He's standing in front of a huge crowd, and people are crying, falling down, and worshiping God. He's only six or seven at the time, and based on this dream his parents could assume that he's called to be an important preacher or evangelist. That may be true, but the very next week, the little boy dreams he's a doctor, and then later he dreams he's in charge of building basements for old ladies who own cats. All of these could be destiny dreams, even though each of them is very different.

Again, even though we may feel strongly about certain dreams they've had, we should not force our children to step into what we feel the dreams are offering. They need to discover their callings for themselves, for that gives each of them a sense of ownership. Then, when the inevitable ups and downs of life come, they will know they are on the course God assigned to them and not simply following their parents' wishes.

When our children have calling dreams, we should pay attention and then respond in wisdom. If there seem to be ways in which we could contribute to their understanding or preparation, we should take them, but we always need to be led by the Holy Spirit.

Prophetic and Revelatory Dreams

Prophetic dreams fall into one of two categories: They can be for another person or group, or they can be personal (telling the dreamer about his or her own future). By definition, they are dreams that reveal things that will occur, or may occur, in the future.

When Steve was about six years old, he rode with his mother to pick up a visiting minister at the airport. As they were driving home, Steve started telling a dream he'd had the night before. It was somewhat epic, with a main character, blue cliffs, three horses, battles, and ultimately victory. The minister immediately knew the dream was for him, and he was so impacted that he sat in the car and wept while young Steve finished speaking. When he had composed himself, he told Steve and his mother that he had been asking God about the future of his ministry. God had told him that he would receive the answer while on this trip. Of course, he had imagined it would come from revelation, another leader, or in the meetings he was scheduled to have. He had not imagined that a little six-year-old boy would carry the key, but God knew.

God will give our children prophetic dreams for other people. Some of them will be positive, as in the previous example. At other times, however, children may have somewhat disturbing, realistic prophetic dreams that frighten them. Such dreams are prophetic calls to intercession, often to prevent a harmful thing from happening. Years ago, a young friend of ours in Great Britain dreamed that a plane exploded and crashed in Scotland. He was very impacted by what he saw; it seemed real to him. Within hours, Pan Am flight 103 crashed in Lockerbie, Scotland. Many of the visual reports in the media bore a distinct resemblance to what he had described to his parents after his dream but before the crash.

After 9/11, many people came up to Greg and showed him journals and pages of notes describing the terrorist attack — dreams they had had before the attack had actually occurred. Some dreams were more symbolic and some were literal, but each of them was amazingly consistent: planes flying into buildings, Middle Eastern men with box cutters, etc. Sometimes the dreamers could identify the buildings, and sometimes they could even identify the planes. In every case, they hadn't understood what the dreams had meant. *Surely, it couldn't be literal*, they thought.

Should they have done something? What could they have done? It is important that we respond to God-given dreams of events like these with prayer and intercession.

While we can't speak for God and why He gives certain dreams to certain people, we do know that He reveals the future to His prophets (Amos 3:7). Intercession is always the best response, especially when we do not have clarity regarding a dream's interpretation.

When children have dreams and other experiences like these, don't allow them to bear any guilt afterward. Our first response should be to pray with them. If it is a tragedy, pray for mercy — that God would intervene and His will would be done. All of us, children and adults alike, have been called to pray for God's will and mercy. If He wants your children to take any further action, He will make sure they, or you, know.

Keep in mind that prophetic and revelatory dreams can also be times of training. God may be showing you or your children in advance what could transpire, so that you cultivate experience and history in prophetic revelation.

Some years ago, Nancy, a friend and pastor's wife, had a dream about an international ministry leader, a man who had been very important to her family. In this dream, the man had fallen into immorality and suffered a horrific tragedy in his life. She knew the dream was from God, and she and her husband began to pray fervently for him.

A year later, this man did fall into immorality. His wife left him, his young son was tragically killed, and the man moved into the New Age community. Our friend was distraught and felt guilty, thinking that she and her husband hadn't done enough to prevent this heartbreak. Later on, however, she learned that several leaders had had the same dream from God, and some of them had gone to this man and implored him to seek help, all to no avail. Our friend then realized that for her, this dream had been a call to intercession, and it had also been training so that she would know with confidence that God was speaking to her in her dreams.

Again, intercession should always be our first response. In time, it may even become a "reflex" for you; when God gives you a dream, you automatically ask Him about it and seek His best outcome.

Intercession Dreams

In intercession dreams, God reveals something to us so that we can pray about it. These dreams may be about present or future events and may or may not be prophetic in nature; they may be about situations your children already know about, such as a sick friend or relative.

Many people call the urge to pray a "burden" because the urge's intensity can cause us to feel heavy and troubled. This is why it is important for your children to understand what to do with intercession dreams: They should pray about them. They shouldn't hold onto the dreams and try to carry them themselves, but they need to give the dreams back to God. If they don't return them to Him, the dreams can drain their strength and even embitter them in the long run.

Not every "burden" is something that will quickly pass. For instance, when children face a severely ill friend or family member, they are going to experience sorrow; that is a normal process they will need to work through, and it is very different than carrying the weight of something God didn't intend for them to carry. Whenever you see your children worrying over or struggling with another person's trouble, explain to them that God wants us to respond to others' dilemmas with compassion, intercession, and assistance when we are able, but we need to pass those burdens back to God. In most cases, we cannot fix others' problems, and God did not mean for us to carry the weight of them ourselves.

As God gives intercession dreams to your children, join them in prayer but then follow their lead. If they seem more inclined to respond to God by themselves (praying alone), step back and let them do that. In times like this, God is building relationship with your children, and as parents, we shouldn't try to be the conduit when they are ready to do things on their own.

Direction Dreams

Joey broke the neighbor's window by accident. He didn't want to get in trouble or have the neighbor think he was bad, so he didn't tell anyone. But a few days later, he had a dream in which his school principal told him he needed to tell his parents what had happened and then go and apologize to the neighbor. It was a very straightforward dream.

It is possible that the principal represented himself in the dream, but in the natural, he didn't know that Joey had broken the window. Even if he had known, it wouldn't have been his place to instruct Joey about something unrelated to school. Most likely, the principal represented God — the only One who actually knew about the window. In other words, by giving little Joey this dream, God was tidying up the situation.

Children will have direction dreams in which God shows them the way they should take, or could take, in a situation that may or may not have transpired yet. Direction dreams are similar to self-condition dreams in that they center on events of the dreamer's life, but then they go a step further by helping the child know what he or she needs to do in response to events.

Healing Dreams

God often uses dreams to tell children what they need to know in order for them to be healed from a past event. The dream itself can bring healing, deliverance, or closure.

Our friend Daniel tells a story about a dream interpretation event at a park. A long line of people waited to have their dreams interpreted, and in the line stood eight-year-old Terry and his mother and sister. Daniel could see that Terry's family was getting tired of standing in line, but the little boy was adamant that he wanted to tell his dream.

Finally it was their turn. Terry told Daniel, "I was asleep in my bed. My dad came to my bed and put his arms around me. He told me that everything was going to be okay and that he would be watching out for me from Heaven. He kissed me. Then he was gone."

The dream was fairly straightforward. Daniel told Terry that his father had obviously not been able to say good-bye. As Daniel was speaking, the mother and sister started crying.

"This is so amazing!" Terry's mother said.

Daniel kind of shrugged and replied, "It was a simple closure dream — where God gives a dream to someone who has lost a loved one and there was no opportunity in the natural for that closure."

But the mother insisted on how amazing it was. "You don't understand. Terry's father died in an accident almost a year ago, and Terry has not looked anyone in the eye since that day."

Daniel looked down, and Terry was looking directly at him. It was evident to everyone that the angst and agony were entirely gone from the little boy's face, and not only Terry but his mother and sister as well were left with greater peace.

This was a closure dream — a type of healing dream that healed all three members of this family. It bore fruit that produced change for everyone involved.

There are many ways God can use dreams to heal. Healing dreams can reveal previously unknown information or understanding that causes us to see painful situations differently. We can forgive others in dreams, discover ways to restore broken relationships, and overcome offenses. God can also use healing dreams to show us how much He loves us, a truth that, when understood, heals many things indeed.

Spiritual Warfare Dreams

Spiritual warfare dreams are often categorized as nightmares for three reasons. First, these dreams typically occur at the enemy's initiation and therefore are black and white, like many nightmares (see the section on colors). Second, the general plot is common to nightmares as well: Something is chasing the children, attacking them, or trying to scare them. Spiritual warfare dreams also tend to generate many of the same emotions as nightmares: fear, anxiety, heightened heart rate, etc.

The primary difference between spiritual warfare dreams and nightmares is that in the former, our children usually prevail — they defeat their enemies and are victorious, while nightmares often bring about the opposite. These dreams are called spiritual warfare dreams because our children's actions against the enemy in the dream are real; they affect and bring change in the spiritual realm, even though they happen while the children are asleep.

Dreams can be excellent training ground for spiritual warfare, as long as the dreams aren't disruptive to the children. They need to know that God is always with them, no matter what they dream or how it made them feel.

We used to tell our children, "Well, the dream must have turned out well, because here you are to recount the story!" In other words, no matter how our children feel after waking up from a spiritual warfare dream, God will prevail, and they can win these wars.

Visions

In addition to dreams, children may also have visions. Since this book isn't an in-depth study of dreams and visions, we will look just at the most basic differences between the two and how they impact children.

Visions may occur during the day while children are awake (these are often referred to as open visions) or at night while they're asleep. Twilight (in between asleep and awake) is also a prolific time for our children to hear clearly from God.

Sometimes, visions are more literal than dreams. Sarah's tornado dream may have been a vision that occurred during a twilight time. But whether it was or wasn't isn't particularly important, since it received the appropriate response and brought about the appropriate outcome — that we would ask God to change our circumstances.

Colors in Dreams

Color (or its absence) in a dream may help reveal the source of the dream. God is light and the source of light, so dreams from God are normally in vivid color. Black-and-white or gray-scale dreams are usually not from God. They sometimes indicate the plans of the enemy, or they can be nightmares. Colors are very symbolic, and often the color will help us identify what the object represents.

When interpreting our children's dreams, one of our primary steps should be to ask if the dream was in black and white or in color. Colors can sometimes be difficult for children to remember, so it is helpful to ask, "What color was the grass (or some other element)?" This may help them focus and better recall the details. If they still aren't certain, it doesn't mean they are confused. It simply means that their attention could be on other parts of the dream rather than the colors.

One of our children, now an adult, was recently talking about this book with some friends, and he said that he can still remember being asked at breakfast, "What did you dream? What colors did you see in your dream?" This helped him in his current understanding of dreams, and it also helped to develop his retention skills.

Following is a list of common colors and what they typically represent. The lists of symbols found in this chapter were taken from John Loren Sandford's *Elijah Among Us* (Chosen, 2002). Please see our Bibliography and Suggested Resources section for more information.

Colors
Positive meaning
Negative meaning

Red
Love, the blood of forgiveness
Anger ("I saw red")

Yellow
Happiness

Cowardice ("a yellow streak")

Gold
Wisdom, nature of God, goodness ("as good as gold")
Miserly, materialism

Blue
Eternity, healing, hope, sky, uplifting feelings
Depression ("singing the blues" or "I'm feeling blue today")

Green
Life, new beginnings, nature
Jealousy ("the green-eyed monster")

Brown
Acceptance, warmth, success, earth, foundations
Disgust, disappointment

Black
Reverence, seriousness, creation; theological meanings: creativity, rebirth, new possibilities, new life
Death, grief, despair, defeat

Purple
Royalty, reigning in power
Rage ("he turned purple")

White
Purity, innocence, unbrokeness
Surrender, fear ("he turned white")

Orange
Dawning of the new day, beauty
Brashness, boldness

Gray/neutral

Mystery, hope obscured in hiddeness
Sadness ("it's a gray day")

Pink
Health, true femininity, good fortune ("in the pink")
Illness, weakness, immaturity, effeminacy

Vehicles in Dreams

Vehicles of any sort (cars, trains, planes, bicycles, etc.) usually represent a person's vocation or ministry, because they take a person from one point to another.

A little eight-year-old who is driving "her" car may be dreaming about the job she will have someday or what her task (sometimes another word for *ministry*) is today. For example, Susan had a dream that she was grown up and on a train with lots of other people. They were going all over the world and filling up warehouses with food and everything people needed. No matter how much they took out of the train, when they got to the next city, the train would be filled again, and they then would stock the warehouse in that city.

This dream may mean that Susan is, or will be, part of a large ministry with an international scope; we know this because the train is going "all over the world." As this ministry does what it is called to do, they will meet the needs (spiritual and/or physical) of people internationally, and God will continuously replenish their resources.

On the negative side, vehicles can refer to something "carrying us away," such as evil thoughts, feelings, or projects that we "ride in." On the positive side, vehicles can represent faith, a belief structure, or a good thought or emotion that carries or motivates us.[1]

Vehicles
Positive meaning
Negative meaning

---

1 Sandford, *Elijah Among Us*

Car
Personal work, ministry, what you are "riding in" emotionally, thinking
What you are "riding in" emotionally, thinking

Bus
Bigger ministry, bigger emotions or thoughts

Airplane
Large church or ministry, large thoughts or emotions

Train
Denomination, movement, large corporation

Moving van
Geographical move

Raft
A saving (as on Noah's ark)
Floundering, adrift

Animals in Dreams

As we've briefly discussed, animals can represent different things to different children according to their personal dream language. This is true of any symbol, but we see it most often with animals. As in our earlier example, if a child is afraid of dogs, dogs probably mean something negative in his or her dreams, but if a child likes dogs, they may represent something positive. What the creatures are doing in the dream can also show us what they represent. For instance, if the dog is chasing the child and trying to bite him or her, that would typically mean something demonic.

Dogs can mean spiritual or physical companions (angelic or demonic company or unbelievers). Horses are similar to vehicles in that they carry people from one location to another, but as they are alive, they tend to represent moves of the Spirit (being carried by God). Horses also represent power and authority. Obviously, monsters (unknown creatures that frighten or attack children) usually represent the enemy.

Animals
Positive meaning
Negative meaning

Snake
Judgment, healing (bronze serpent in Numbers 21:9)
Rebelliousness, cleverness, hidden enemy ("snake in the grass")

Horse
Strength, beauty, free spirit, a philosophy or emotion to ride on
Pride in fleshly strength ("riding a dead horse"), foreboding (four horsemen of the Apocalypse)

Bear
Courage to stand and fight, protectiveness ("mother bear")
Rage, something that attacks, a difficult situation

Dog
Watchdog, conscience, loyal ("man's best friend")
Unbeliever, outsider, ugly

Cat
Gracefulness, speed, strategy
Slinking, treachery, ambush, spiteful ("catty")

Lion
Jesus (the Lion of Judah), regal, protection, courage, strength ("lionhearted")
Satan (or a demon) ravages, devours

Numbers in Dreams
Unlike symbols, phrases, and other elements that have cultural

meaning, numbers usually translate smoothly from one language to another. In most cases, the attributed meaning of a number is based on its first usage in Scripture.

Numbers
Meaning

1
God

2
Multiplication or division

3
Trinity (Father. Son, Holy Spirit)

4
Earth, creation, world

5
Grace

6
People (humanity), or beast, Satan

7
God's perfection, completeness

8
New beginnings, resurrection

9
Fruitfulness, finality

10
Trial, testing, law, order, government

11
Transition, incomplete

12
Divine government, apostolic

13
Rebellion

30
Maturity, beginning of ministry, consecration

50
Jubilee, Pentecost

Activities in Dreams

Flying in a dream usually represents operating in the supernatural.

Teeth typically represent discernment, so when we dream that ours are falling out, it could mean that we are losing our ability to see or discern spiritually. Children will have dreams about this from time to time, but remember that for children, losing teeth is a common occurrence, so these dreams may speak about timing. If they dream that they lose a tooth and that their teacher is moving away, it could be that the teacher's moving is the point of the dream. God is letting the children know what is going to happen and when.

Dreams about taking showers or baths generally represent being cleansed from things that have impacted us from the outside — i.e., from the world.

Activities
Positive meaning
Negative meaning

Asleep
Rest
Spiritual indifference

Awake
Alertness, watching

Dance
Joy, rejoicing

Singing
Praise

Walk
Your life, how you conduct yourself

Locations in Dreams

Where did the dream take place? This can provide the dream's context. Dreams that take place in the children's home tend to be about their personal lives, while dreams involving hotels may be about transitions (people don't usually stay in hotels for long periods of time). Dreams that take place at home churches probably represent ministries or spiritual activities that involve the church body, and dreams that take place at Dad's office or place of employment are probably about work the Father is doing.

Hallways or tunnels usually symbolize a transition, and the length of the hallway or tunnel may indicate how long the transition will last.

Locations
Positive meaning
Negative meaning

Attic
History (of individual or family)

Bed or couch
Rest

Closet
Private information, personal details

Door
Entrance to something new, opportunity

River or sea
Holy Spirit (Your depth in the water may reflect your depth in the things of God)

Dry riverbed
Religion, barrenness

People in Dreams

As we have said, certain people can be highly symbolic in dreams. People who appear in our dreams over and over again could represent authority, God, spiritual covering, etc. For example, a Captain would most likely represent some kind of authority, possibly Jesus. A shepherd will often represent Jesus as well. The context of the dream is very important.

When we dream about people we don't know in real life but they seem to be our friends in the dream, we may be dreaming about angelic beings. This is especially true if we can't see or don't recognize their faces. Knowing what these beings are doing in the dream is a large part of understanding the dream. At other times, people we don't know in our dreams are people we will meet later. The dream (or dreams) is in preparation for the meeting.

We have included these symbols to help you get started on interpreting your dreams, or your child's dream. Keep in mind though that no list of symbols will give you a dream interpretation. Today, I hear many people who are very good at identifying the symbols in dreams, but they may not always be as good at interpreting the dream because they are operating out of information alone, rather than with revelation and information. You must have Holy Spirit revelation to interpret a dream from God.

People
Positive meaning
Negative meaning

Baby
Birthing of a new thought, idea, or development, call to prayer for blessing or protection
Bad is being started, warning to stop something

Man
Friendship ("company coming"), faith, good logic, initiative, strength
Enemy approaching, no guard over logic

Woman
Nurture, beauty, intuitive, feeling side of us, the Church
Seduction, weakness, hyperemotional fulfillment

Father
Authority, protection, discipline, faith and belief structure, caring, bring forth light
Fear of authority, overbearing, controlling, domineering, too logical

Mother
Affection, sweetness, nurture, intuitive side
Fear of criticism and control, emotional control of us

Dead person
Calling for a good kind of crucifixion, person, project, emotion, etc.
Warning that good is dying, such as person, projection, emotion, etc.

Keeping a Journal

We know an intelligent, relatively literate seven-year-old boy who has kept multiple dream journals. Sometimes when we visit his family, he will bring out a journal and share one or two dreams with us. It is an adventure for him and seems to be as good as any book he can get at a bookstore. As this continues and he grows into adulthood, he won't have any trouble believing that God speaks to him through his dreams — he has volumes of written proof.

Journaling dreams is especially important for children, for it will emphasize that we, their parents, think dreams are important, and it will also help cultivate their gift for dreaming. We don't need to wait for our young children to reach a certain age before introducing them to this activity. If they haven't learned to write yet, someone can help them (perhaps you or an older sibling). In this way, nothing is lost or dismissed, and their training can begin at an early age.

Another value to journaling is that it helps capture additional details that our children might have missed or forgotten. It also reveals nuances and perspectives. Over time, we'll be able to see emerging patterns (the development of their personal dream language, reoccurring fears, calling dreams, blessings God has for them, etc.) and know how to better assist our children in those specific areas.

Many dreamers come to realize that there is a pattern to their dream life and that they tend to have specific kinds of dreams or special dreams in certain seasons or on certain days of the year. For instance, we know some men of God who have special experiences around the Day of Atonement. These patterns may take years to recognize, but awareness of them is part of understanding and receiving.

Different Ways to Journal Dreams

Most of us are accustomed to journaling in straightforward recitation. This is the most common way to journal dreams and whatever else God may speak to us. There are several different ways we can journal, however, and it can be helpful to use different methods for different dreams.

For instance, many dreams can be expressed well as drawings. Some children might be more adept at communicating with pictures rather than words. In this case, let them use a three-ring binder instead of a bound journal, which gives them the liberty to draw or paint pictures, make collages, or otherwise record the dream. The point is to record what God has shown them; the actual form or method of recording isn't as important.

For certain dreams, using timelines or diagrams can be helpful. Experiment with different methods for different dreams and in the end do what seems right for each dream. Before long, you will be able to tell which method works best for each dream.

On an organizational note, if you have a written story of the dream and a coinciding picture, timeline, or diagram, keep both together. Also, always date the dream. It can be very useful to use a date format such as this: "Saturday, March 1, 2008, 6:00 a.m." This way, dreamers may begin to recognize patterns in the day of the week, or the month of the year, and realize that they have certain types or topics of dreams at specific times. They also may recognize that they have more dreams at four o'clock or midnight, instead of closer to the morning.

Help your children title each dream. This simple step can be very illuminating because it helps them express what stood out to them about the dream. Obviously, a title also helps locate the dream if they need to look it up later.

If your children don't seem to remember very much

about a specific dream, by asking questions you can help them pull out more details. "What did the man look like? What was he wearing? Did you have anything with you?" At the same time, however, be careful not to lead the children. Their imaginations can be highly vivid, and if they think you want extra details, that can muck things up.

In Conclusion

We sleep about a third of our lives. If we don't believe dreams can be from God, that is a lot of time to be disconnected from His voice! God will often speak to our children in dreams. As parents, there will be times when we are stunned by the significance of what He communicates to them while they are sleeping.

Those little dreams that are so obvious today may turn out to mean something different, larger, or more important than we initially thought. Some dreams are seeds planted in the child's spirit that will not come to bloom for decades.

God knows what He is doing and why He gives each specific child his or her own specific dreams. Simply put, what we know today is what we need to know today, and it shouldn't worry us if we can't answer all of our children's dream questions, or if we don't yet have tomorrow's wisdom or understanding. It will come when it's needed.

For more information on learning how to interpret your dreams or your children's dreams, visit www.raisingspiritual-children.com

Something to Ponder

Brilliant Dreamers

Children love to see how God puts two and two together, and they are often delighted to learn how many "discoveries" have come through dreams. To encourage your children's faith and their interest in dreams, go over the list below with them and add to it as you learn of more examples. All of these inventions and discoveries came about because of dreams.

Music — Paul McCartney first heard the tune of "Yesterday" in a dream.

Nobel Peace Prize — Otto Loewi (1873–1961), a German-born physiologist, won the Nobel Prize for medicine in 1936 for his work on the chemical transmission of nerve impulses. He had dreamed about a certain experiment that proved his hypothesis.[1]

Invention — Elias Howe had been working on an automatic stitching machine, and although he had tried many different configurations, he was unable to make any of them work. One night he had a dream about a tribe of natives who took him prisoner. They were surrounding him with spears that had holes near the ends. When he woke up from the dream, he realized that he had been putting the holes in the needles in the wrong place. He changed the design, and it worked. He invented the sewing machine in 1845.[2]

1 *Perspectives in Biology and Medicine*, Vol IV, issue 1, page 17
2 Kaempffert, ed., page 385

Golf Swing — Jack Nicklaus, a professional golfer, was having a bad slump in the 1960s. One night he dreamed that he was having great success. When he woke up, he realized that in the dream he had been holding his club in a different way. He went out to practice, held the club as he had in the dream, and became very successful.[3]

Antiaircraft Gun — D.B. Parkinson, an engineer, was designing telephones for Bell Labs in 1940. One night, he had a dream in which he was on the Allied Front in Europe. He noticed that a certain type of gun successfully brought down every plane it targeted. A soldier beckoned him to come closer, and he saw that a mechanism he had been working on for telephones was attached to this gun. He told his superiors at Bell Labs about his dream, and this led to the development of the M9 gun. In a single week in August 1944, M9s were credited with destroying eighty-nine V-1 buzz bombs launched from the Antwerp area toward England.[4]

Mathematics — Rene Descartes had a dream on November 10, 1619, that gave him a deeper understanding of mathematics. This established him as a key figure in the Scientific Revolution.[5]

3 Jack Nicklaus, as told to a *San Francisco Chronicle* reporter; June 27, 1964
4 Schindler, *New Scientist*, page 53
5 Davis and Hersh, *Descartes' Dream*

Chapter 10

Stopping Your Children's Nightmares

Some children seem to experience more than their share of nightmares and other nighttime terrors. Have you ever wondered why?

Nightmares or bad dreams are distressing events for both children and adults; however, they can be therapeutic in that they may reveal a forgotten or suppressed trauma. By exposing the trauma or dark experience, the power of that darkness is considerably weakened.

Even though a closed shoebox is full of darkness, once we take the lid off, the darkness disappears; it cannot keep the light out. So it is with hidden, suppressed, or forgotten trauma. When your children tell you about their nightmares, it is important to listen and discern whether the enemy is coming to discourage and frighten them, or whether there is an issue, recent or long past, whose time has come to be exposed.

Nightmares, both for children and adults, may also be attacks purposefully meant to generate fear, anxiety, grief, and other harmful emotions. They are a strategy of the enemy to train children out of dreaming. If he can cause our children to reject their dream lives early on, he will have eliminated one of the primary ways God speaks to them.

As terrifying and unrelenting as nightmares can seem, they are not impossible to overcome. They can be stopped, for God is stronger than anything the enemy could throw at us. That is a fact of our faith, one of the many points of no contention, and because both we and our children can walk in His authority, none of us has to live in fear. In this chapter, we're going to be discussing different ways we can help our children overcome fears in the night.

Changing the Dream While in the Dream

When our young friend Derrick was about nine years old, he was walking upstairs to get ready for bed. It was nighttime, and the only light on in the house was the television downstairs. As he walked into his bedroom, he looked up and saw a demon standing beside his bed, waiting for him. The room was almost pitch black, but he could see the demon because it appeared blacker than the shadows around it, as if its body was absorbing the darkness. Its eyes were a faint reddish color.

As soon as Derrick locked eyes with the spirit, he shouted, "Jesus!" Immediately, the demon burst into a cloud of smoke and was gone.

This little boy had a hands-on encounter with the power of Jesus' name. One of the first things we need to realize about nightmares is that whether we're awake or asleep, the spiritual world works the same. Our bodies sleep, but our spirits do not. In other words, when the enemy attacks our children, they can order him to stop in Jesus' name, and he will. Rebuking the enemy while they're asleep will have the same affect as when they're awake. Dreaming doesn't inhibit God's power.

As soon as they are old enough to understand, we need to teach our children that God is more powerful than any nightmare they could have and that He can put a stop to the dream itself or to the terrifying elements it contains.

As a child, Hazel dreamed that she and her friends were captured by soldiers who wanted to feed them to a giant. They were terrified, but then Hazel suddenly became aware that the situation wasn't real life — it was a dream. She told one of her friends, "I know this is a dream, so I'm going to wake myself up."

Her friend started arguing with her. "No, this is real!" But Hazel knew it was a dream and prayed over and over again that Jesus would wake her up, which He did.

No matter how intense, vivid, and real a nightmare seems, God is stronger. If we can convey His power and limitlessness to our children at an early age, they will have won a huge battle, and they will have won it decades before most people.

Before they go to sleep, have them instruct their spirits to rebuke any dreams coming from the enemy. If a nightmare then tries to come, their spirits will rise up and rebuke the enemy and stop the nightmare. Sometimes children remember that the rebuke happened and sometimes they don't, but you will recognize that your children are now sleeping through the night.

Nightmares Can Be Training Times
Rebuking the enemy in dreams isn't always done with words. Dreams are metaphorical, which means that our children may sometimes battle the monster or "bad guy" hand to hand. Perhaps we see this with our boys especially! We shouldn't be concerned when they tell us of their fighting dreams, because those dreams can be metaphorical representations of rebuking the enemy.

Children are often thrilled to find that in the midst of battle, they can destroy what has come to destroy them.

Young Carl was being hounded by nightmares. Every time his parents prayed for him, the nightmares would lessen for a while, but then they would return just as strong as they had been before. One night, however, they stopped.

Carl came into the kitchen the next morning and announced, "There was a witch in my bed last night."

"What did you do?" his dad asked him.

"Oh, I killed her," Carl said.

Being helpful, his dad said, "If that ever happens again, you can speak to her and tell her to leave in Jesus' name."

Carl replied, "No, if it ever happens again, I'm going to kill her again!"

While nightmares are the enemy's weapon to destroy peace, generate fear, and discourage dreaming or valuing dreams, God may occasionally allow such dreams for a child's training. Carl knew who he was in God, and God used the spirit of might He'd given the boy to destroy what was repeatedly attacking him.

Night Terrors

Have you ever been harassed in the night? We know many children (and adults) who have awakened in the middle of the night and sensed that something evil was in the room. They were terrified, may have felt a pressure or constraint on their chests, and usually were not able to speak.

When this happens, it isn't "just our imagination." Something specific has come to torment us.

We need to train our children that if this happens (or if they dream it's happening), all they have to do is speak Jesus' name (audibly or in their thoughts), tell the demon to leave, and it will. It is an incredibly empowering experience for our children when they recognize that this thing that seemed larger than life actually is very much under their authority.

Nine-year-old Lila had a dream about walking upstairs and seeing a demon outside her bedroom. It had white skeletal features and looked very frightening. But when the demon saw Lila, it started running away — not the other way around! Demons are more aware of God's authority in our lives than we are. If we can train our children to walk in that authority, fear won't be something they have to deal with — in any issue, whether asleep or awake.

Children's Dreams and Family Lifestyles

If your children are having repeated nightmares, it could be that something in the children's everyday life is causing them. Don't overlook the obvious. If there seems to be a recurring event or person troubling your children's dreams, look at what that person is doing in the natural and see if you can see the parallel.

Perhaps there is something you can change or remove, and that will then stop the nightmares.

If that doesn't work, perhaps you should start looking into someone else's life: yours.

Many years ago when we worked in deliverance ministry, we learned that in order to deliver the children, we first needed to deliver the parents. In most cases, that would remove or heal the family's problems, and we subsequently would not need to minister to the children themselves.

As parents, we have a great deal of control over harassing dreams or nightmares. Our young children are under authority, and if nightmares or night terrors are problems in your home, look for patterns both in your children's lives and in *your* life.

Are you in a season of spiritual warfare that is unusually strong for you? Have you somehow left your children uncovered? Has something happened that might have given an opening for the enemy? Are the movies or video games being watched and played in the house crossing over into questionable areas? Are you struggling with jealousy, envy, strife, or selfish ambition? How about unforgiveness? All of these things can open doors to the enemy (James 3:16).

Again, nightmares and night terrors are not something that we or our children have to live with. They are not just "a part of life." Our God is the God of Peace, and He never intended for us to be subject to the enemy. Therefore, we shouldn't let the enemy lull us into complacency and steal from our families. Peace and rest come from God, and we should not let the enemy take them from us.

Purifying Property

Finally, if you have tried everything you can think of and still have had little to no success, it could be that your house or property has residual spirits. The following story exemplifies this.

A friend of ours, Amanda, grew up in a house that her

parents had bought quite some time before she was born. It was an old house with a lot of history; it had been a part of the Underground Railroad system, and a tunnel connected it to a house at the end of the block. This meant that a lot of fear had once traveled through that house.

The woman who had last owned the house was a known witch. She had been prolific in occult activity and had had a public affair with a married man. Amanda's parents were aware of these things, but they weren't aware of their need to take authority over what they owned and command any residual darkness to leave. The power of God is stronger than that of the enemy, but if darkness was once allowed to live in your place of residence, you need to take measures to "un-invite" it, as it were.

Because that had never been done, Amanda was a happy child during the day and an absolutely terrified child by night. When the lights turned out, the terrors began. She would see demons with their heads cut off, mummies, and other things she sensed might be spiritual beings but thought were only hallucinations. When she closed her eyes, she would see graphically frightening or sexual images. She had trouble sleeping by herself until she was thirteen and couldn't be intimate with God, because she had become terrified that, as a spiritual being, He was going to sexually abuse her. She can remember being as young as three years old and having shocking sexual thoughts, and in order to fall asleep, she would finally just shut down in shame.

While growing up, Amanda never told anyone what was happening. People said that she had an active imagination, and she assumed that everyone could "see" the way she could (a very common but erroneous assumption that many children make). Years later, through counseling and spiritual mentorship, she was able to realize what had been happening to her as a child and why, and then receive healing.

Your place of residence is yours. You have authority over it. If nightmares are an issue in your home, take authority over your entire house. You can declare in the house, and out-side of it if appropriate, that you have authority over that house and it is dedicated to God. As it says in Joshua 24:15, "But as for me and my family, we will serve the Lord." This declaration lets the spiritual world know that the house is under God's rule and authority, and evil cannot trespass without serious conse-quences. If Amanda's parents had taken these steps and cleansed their property, they would have saved their daughter years of fear and shame.

Are there are any lingering spiritual residues in your house? Who lived there before you did? Did the previous occu-pants dabble in witchcraft, or was there domestic abuse? The demonic entities associated with evil activities and motivations usually remain in the house — until they are driven out.

As a symbolic act, you may want to anoint with oil the outside and inside edges, as well as the doors and windows, of the house you are dedicating to God. Doing symbolic and prophetic acts like this with your children will add to their tan-gible history with God, for these are good examples of how God is ever present in all aspects of our lives. It also will show them that even though you are strong and capable parents, you submit yourselves to God and acknowledge that He has authority over all things. You may already verbally communi-cate that in many ways to your children, but showing it to them is invaluable.

When I (Patricia) travel, I often use a similar variation of property cleansing to get a good night's sleep. I routinely cleanse my hotel rooms of any demonic presences or residues. Also, hotels can be noisy places, especially in a big city, so before I go to sleep, I tell my spirit that I don't want to be dis-turbed by revelry in the hallway or the traffic outside on the street. This leaves me open to waking up in an emergency but also gives me a good night's sleep. The result is that I rarely lose sleep in a hotel, and I wake up when I want to.

I also decide when I want to get up. Waking up without an alarm is beneficial because alarm clocks, though sometimes necessary, are very disruptive. Much revelation, including many dreams, comes in the last of our twilight sleep — right before we wake up. An alarm clock at the end of a dream or night vision will sometimes cause the dream to be lost. By waking up naturally, we are apt to remember the dream or vision more clearly. Just to be careful, I will sometimes set an alarm if I must be up at a certain time, but I purpose to wake up ten minutes or so before the alarm goes off.

In Conclusion

All of our authority comes from God. He is so much stronger than anything that could ever come against us. This understanding is one of the first steps to ridding our home of nightmares. When children fully grasp God's power and their authority, they will be able to stand against the enemy. Though frightening elements may still enter their dreams every once in a while, our children will no longer suffer nightmare after nightmare.

This knowledge of God will affect their dreams. It will also affect their waking lives and allow them to live in greater peace overall.

Something to Ponder

Ponder a Picture . . .

God often speaks in pictures, symbols, and metaphors. This is evidenced in many ways but specifically in the ancient language of His people. Ancient Hebrew was pictographic; instead of writing words phonetically, the Hebrews constructed words with symbols and pictures.

Dreams, visions, and spiritual experiences are other areas in which we often see metaphors and symbols in action. Understanding God and growing in relationship with Him sometimes require us to think and look pictorially. There are many things that we can do to help our children (and ourselves) expand our perceptions of the spiritual realm:

1. Study Jesus' parables. For example, the parable of the sower in Luke 8 has a number of symbols: the rocks, the weeds, being stepped on, the birds, etc. What did Jesus say these items represented? Western education often encourages our children to think literally, but exploring parables, metaphors, and symbolism will help them develop all aspects of cognition, including metaphorical understanding.

A beneficial component of parables and storytelling is that children tend to recognize symbolism right away, and if something isn't readily understandable, we usually can help them discover understanding.

2. Read books that are allegorical and symbolic in nature, such as *The Spirit Flyer Series* by John Bibee (InterVarsity Press). In a clear and interesting way, these books portray the spiritual

realm, good, evil, and the devious ways the enemy tries to trick us. They are especially great books to read aloud as a family. When Greg read these books to our children, we tried to limit ourselves to one chapter a night, but he sometimes wasn't able to put the book down. The kids were so captivated by the story that they often took the books off the shelf and read ahead themselves.

3. Learn to ask, "Why?" Why did God say that *birds* came and ate the seeds instead of, say, a dog licking them up? (Have you ever noticed that kids find something fascinating about dogs licking things up? Why is that?) Remember, the process is important. Even if you think an answer is obvious, searching it out may still have value for you and your children.

4. Prompt your kids to pay attention not only to what is said but also to what isn't said. In Numbers 13, God could have corrected the ten who didn't want to go out and take the Promised Land; He could have made them go. Why didn't He do that? What He didn't do is as important to understand as what He did do.

5. Model and nurture pondering, thinking, and meditating to your children. Culturally, we tend to want the answer (or interpretation or understanding) immediately, but God's ways are not always the ways of our culture. In fact, they usually aren't. Gathering information is not as valuable as developing understanding. "Don't just sit there and do nothing" makes sense to a parent who is on the go and busy, but it can also be just plain wrong. For example, sitting on the carpet and noticing all the different colors or shapes or lengths of fiber is not "nothing." At certain times, doing "nothing" is much, much more important than doing "something." If there is too much to do at your house, perhaps you should re-evaluate what you are doing and reprioritize so that there is time and space for important things, like sitting on the swing and imagining.

Chapter 11

Take Courage

*We are only as good as the courage we have to act
according to our beliefs.*
— Greg Mapes

The other day, five-year-old Cody dropped the milk carton. It hit the freshly mopped kitchen floor and burst open, sloshing milk across the linoleum and even the cat. Cody's mom had already experienced a series of setbacks that day, and when he dropped the milk, she lost it and yelled at him. She was so upset that she almost couldn't control herself. Afterward, she felt terrible. She regretted what she had said and wanted to make it right.

As we mentioned in Chapter 1, raising children is much harder than it looks from the outside. No matter how hard we've studied, tried, attempted, and worked to perfect ourselves, all of us will occasionally miss the mark or fall short. This is one reason that we, as parents, need to be able to tell the difference between conviction (from the Holy Spirit) and condemnation (from the enemy). When faced with our shortcomings, how will we react? Will we be able to continue forward, knowing that God's opinion of us hasn't changed? Or will we want to give up? The enemy's voice often masquerades as our own thoughts, so at first, conviction and condemnation can seem like one and the same. However, once we understand and learn to recognize the differences, the two will be much easier to tell apart — if not in the moment, then at least eventually.

Conviction is distinct, known, and solvable. It may bring regret, but it also brings hope, because we know that even though we have erred, there is a way out of it. Under conviction, Cody's mother would remember that her son was only five years old and was acting his age. She would know she had made a mistake and that she needed to go to her son and ask for his forgiveness. Yes, she had done wrong — but all she needed to do now was this one thing, and then the situation would be righted. As Job 11:18 says, "'Having hope will give you courage.'"

Condemnation, on the other hand, makes us feel incredibly hopeless, heavy, and weary, and it does not offer a way out. Under condemnation, Cody's mother would think, *I am such a bad mother! I never do anything right. I can't keep up, and there is no way my kids will have a chance at a good life. I should just give up now.* These thoughts are not from God. As true as they may seem in the face of apparent failure, they have nothing to do with Him. He is the God of Hope, and so He always allows for hope; He always gives a way out (1 Corinthians 10:13) when we have sinned. *Do this,* He speaks to our hearts, *and it will be done. I can handle the rest.*

One of the enemy's goals is to stop you and your children from reaching God's purposes for your lives, and he will often attempt to do this by overwhelming you. Show your children what freedom from sin looks like by not agreeing with the enemy's lies — and be certain your children don't agree with them, either. Nothing will cut off the enemy's plans like adorning your children with affirmation, grace, and love.

If you can tell the difference between conviction and condemnation, you will also be able to tell the difference between signals coming from God (revelation) and signals coming from other sources. The words of God bring life. Whenever He speaks to us, we are happier, lighter, and better off than we were before, even if He is bringing correction. This is possible because He is love (1 John 4:8). Therefore, we can know we are

hearing His voice based on how He approaches us, the rele-
vance of what He shares with us, and the fruit that is produced
from what we hear.[1] If we are receiving "revelation" that doesn't
line up with these three criteria, we should put it on the shelf
(wait for God to clarify it) or ignore it.

As parents, we need to apply these three tests to everything we are hearing and sensing so that we can help our children do the same. We need to stop accepting condemnation
and resolve today that while we are not perfect, we are part of
God's perfect design and are intended to have major impact in
our children's lives. Although we will occasionally fall short, He
is able to keep us standing (Romans 14:4; Jude 1:24).

Courage can be a difficult thing to summon up after
we have sinned and are struggling to forgive ourselves, but
whenever we have the strength to take God at His word, we
will find freedom.

Courage Enables Expressions of Love

Years ago, I (Patricia) was speaking at a conference, and a man
I held in very high regard was a speaker at the same conference.
He told me he was coming to hear me that morning, and in my
heart I thought, *Oh, no . . . Please don't do that.* Of course, I
smiled and didn't say anything like that, but I was intimidated
and felt inadequate as a speaker compared to him.

Before the morning session began, I scoped out the
room and saw that this man wasn't there, much to my relief.
However, just a few minutes into my teaching, he and his entire
entourage walked in. My heart sank, but right then, I felt God
say to me, "Patty, step into your calling!"

Immediately, I felt great strength. I took one step to the
side so that the lectern was not in front of me and then took one
big step forward. It was a prophetic act, a response to God, and
where my public speaking and teaching are concerned, I have
never looked back from that moment. While I endeavor to grow
and improve in what I'm doing, I know that as I step forward,
God will help me get to where I need to be. I don't always know

1 Lord, *Hearing God*, Chapter 3

how to proceed, but He does. All I need to do is have courage and step forward willingly.

An often-ignored aspect of life is that we can walk with God for decades but still miss our destinies because of fear. This is what the Israelites did, and they consequently spent a long time in the wilderness. It was courage that separated Joshua and Caleb from the other ten men. Undoubtedly the ten had their reasons and made an eloquent and impassioned presentation to the rest of the Israelites, but their fear prevented them from entering the Promised Land; it kept them from walking into their destinies.

When we submit ourselves to God, He will provide for us. This is a promise and an expectation, not just a wishful thought. If God met Israel day and night for forty years after they had declined His Promised Land, He is certainly going to meet you and your children, whom He has given you. Muster the courage to step into your destiny, and He will provide everything else. As parents, we are in a place of leadership in our families, so it is time for us to have courage and be bold. Don't miss your destiny — and don't let your children miss theirs because you chose to believe the enemy instead of God.

Through the years, we have seen so many men and women who believe in and say the right things, but they don't have the courage to push those principles into action. How many times have you heard of public Christian leaders who slammed immorality from the pulpit, only to be exposed in that same immorality later on? In the wake of these exposures, moral indignation sweeps through the rest of us — but usually not much courage. We want righteousness and love to prevail in our homes, businesses, or organizations, but in the moment of testing, when positions, reputations, ambitions, or money are on the line, too many of us are silent, hoping for the best but not wanting to risk ourselves for righteousness.

Courage is the result of faith, hope, love, and strong character. It allows us to believe God when He speaks of "impossible" things that are about to become reality. It allows us to hope, and it also allows us to love others. Think about your favorite stories, movies, and novels — love battles for what it has chosen. It causes us to speak up for those who cannot speak for themselves. It covers. It fills in the cracks. It is courageous. Let your children grow in courage, pressing beyond the boundaries of their previous accomplishments. Let them learn the joy of risking failure and grow in the relationships that can be birthed as they let their guard down. In order for our children to become what God has called them to become, courage is needed.

Last but not least, courage also enables and urges us to pray.

Praying For Your Children

Ever since they were small, Greg has prayed for our children to grow in wisdom and comprehension beyond their years. He prays this every day. Whenever our children truly amaze me, I hear that prayer ringing in my ears, and I know that we as parents don't need to know everything in order for our children to reach their destinies; we just need to stay in touch and respond to the One who does know everything.

As this book draws to a close, there is a final subject we need to bring to the forefront — something that holds the capability of filling in the cracks and holes left by our mistakes, of strengthening us when we've done all we can, and of proving once again that God is with us. That subject is prayer.

Most of us have heard over and over again that the power of prayer should never be underestimated. But even though we "know" this, it is hard to remember in day-to-day living, and whenever God answers our prayers, many of us find ourselves having to relearn what we thought we already knew:

"For everyone who asks, receives."
— Matthew 7:8

"You can pray for anything, and if you have faith,

you will receive it."
— Matthew 21:22

*"Yes, ask me for anything in my name, and I will
do it!"*
— John 14:14

Carrying our requests and concerns before God in prayer brings about change. This is more than simply a hope; it is a promise. In order for our children to grow into strong men and women who possess good character, know who they are and what they believe in, and are bold enough to follow God with all their hearts, we need to pray for them continually (1 Thessalonians 5:17).

Prayer is more than something followers of God are "just supposed" to do; it is our communion with Him — a heart-to-heart conversation that flows out of our relationship with Him. Conversing (praying) with God should become an automatic response within us, a habit we do on impulse just as we do it automatically with our spouses, children, or friends. Our communion with God nurtures our relationship with Him, which then nurtures communion with Him and so on. It becomes an upward spiral that perpetually increases and strengthens everything we share with the One who loves us.

Part of this communion should be done in front of our children. Family devotions are excellent, but in addition to those times of corporate prayer, our children need to see us spending time with God alone, when it is just Him and us. They need to see us pray and hear us carrying on conversations with Him, asking Him questions and then waiting for His response. We show our children what is important by where we place our attention. If they see that we value our personal prayer times, they will learn that personal prayer times are important. You can spend a few minutes talking to God, reading the Bible, or doing other quiet time activities at the kitchen table where they can see you. You don't need to spend all of your prayer times in the line of sight, but a few minutes on a regular basis will mean so much for your children and their relationship with God.

Another way we can promote prayer in our households is by praying for "small" things, such as where the dog buried the remote control or for extra money for a vacation. When our children observe us doing this, they will learn that God cares for them personally — that He is interested in all their details. The opposite is also true. If our children observe us pray only for "important" things like wisdom for our leaders and healing for the sick, they may assume that God isn't interested in everything they're interested in, and a slight, subtle rift will be constructed. *This is my life over here,* they may think, *and over there are the things I can talk to God about.* Prayer is an excellent way for us to help them understand that nothing is outside of God's notice (Matthew 10:29).

When the boys were small, I (Patricia) took them to the travel agent's office to pick up some tickets. When we came out, I couldn't find my keys. We looked all over the van, emptied my purse, checked inside the office, and searched the ground between the van and the building. Some of the employees even came out to help, but the keys had simply disappeared.

Finally, Zach, who was about six or seven at the time, said, "I don't understand why we aren't doing what we always do — just asking God."

Though I felt a little embarrassed, we stopped (kids and travel agents included) and prayed right there. When we opened our eyes, the keys were on the ground right in front of us, in the middle of the circle we were standing in.

God loves us, and His answers to our prayers will reveal that fact over and over and over again. We need to raise our children with the understanding that His love extends far past outer shells to touch even the hidden things within us. Our hopes matter to Him. Our dreams, our desires, and our wishes are all set before Him — constantly. This is yet another reason His voice always brings us life and not condemnation (Romans 8:1).

In Conclusion

One of the most powerful moments of my life occurred the night our house burned down. After everyone was out of the building, a crowd gathered on the street, and we watched the fire rage in front of us. People were screaming, and sirens were shrill in the background. In the midst of the shock and pandemonium, I was sure that I was losing my mind. In fact, in a surreal, detached sort of way, I thought I could see it leaving me. *Oh,* I thought, *this is what happens when people say they "lost their mind." It really just leaves.*

Greg was horribly burned, and I didn't know if he was going to live. As he collapsed in front of me, he spoke the most powerful words I've ever heard anyone speak. In the slow motion of crisis, he said in a strong voice, "Patty, God is with us!"

This was not something he had intellectually deciphered over years of Bible study and ministry; it was something that his spirit knew. What he said that early morning came from the depths of his being.

When Greg spoke those words, everything seemed to fall back into place. All the screaming around us stopped, and an unearthly peace dropped across the street.

God is with us. None of us are smart or capable enough to do this (life, child rearing, business, education, success) on our own. Therefore, if we want to succeed with our children, we have to rely on the One who is capable. As you walk down this path, reach up, take God's hand, and don't let go. Let Him be the Father that He wants to be for you. Then with your other hand, reach down and take hold of your children. This three-way relationship is what will enable you to become the parent you need to be. God is with you on this journey.

We know that your days are busy and the demands on your time are great. That being the case, we are humbled that you have taken the time to read this book, and our prayer is that it has been more than worthwhile. Be strong and of good courage. May God give you wisdom and comprehension for the road ahead — and a greater portion of love and mercy than you have ever experienced.

> *"So be strong and courageous! Do not be afraid and*
> *do not panic before them. For the LORD your God*
> *will personally go ahead of you. He will neither fail*
> *you nor abandon you."*
> — Deuteronomy 31:6

Something to Ponder

Choose Happiness!

These days, most of us tend to think we are "happy" only when something external is going well. This means that when external events are not coalescing in the perfect cosmic pattern, we are not happy.

That mindset is entirely wrong. Our happiness is ours, and how much of it we have at any given moment is our choice.

I (Patricia) was very young when I had one of the great revelations of my life. When I was six or seven, I was the recipient of a beautiful mahogany Steinway grand piano, which my grandfather had bought in 1911. Grampa Mathewson had it moved to my parents' house with the understanding that I would take lessons on it.

I generally liked playing the piano and found it to be a great adventure. The piano came to represent so much that was right in the world, even though all that practice occasionally seemed "untimely" to my young self. It would, in fact, sometimes make me a little grumpy. However, in my own six-year-old way, I discovered that I could not play the piano and stay grumpy.

Let's face it: There are times when we feel entitled to wear our mad, unhappy expressions and make sure everyone else sees that we're wearing them. If we want to live in happiness, it is important to find what makes us happy.

I tested it and tried it and determined that, at least for me, I could not play the piano and stay in a pouty place. As I grew up, I realized that I could use this to my advantage. I would sit down at the piano when I wanted to lift off those feelings of pain or despair or general unhappiness.

Of course, my family recognized the benefits of this as well. My mother would sometimes walk by as I was struggling over one thing or another and suggest that I play a few pieces. *Can't solve your math problems? Play a few pieces. Feeling left out? Play a few pieces . . .*

Many activities will impact us in a similar way, although there are some aspects of music that speak to our spirits very directly. Our daughter Anna used to skip. When she was happy, she would skip — in the house, at the school, up and down the hall. Before I saw her face, I would know by her gait how she was feeling. One time when she was little, I asked her if she was skipping because she was happy. She told me that you couldn't skip if you weren't happy. I wasn't sure which had come first for her — happiness or skipping — but I suspected she'd had her own revelation.

Questions:

1. What consistently lifts your spirits, whether you want it to or not? Discover what works for you and use it to make every day a better day. Singing? Painting? Dancing? Exercising?

2. However unaware of it they may be, what do your children do that lifts their spirits and overcomes that grumpy thing that was trying to grab a hold of them? If you can see it, enjoy it. As my mother did with me, you may sometimes need to suggest it to them!

3. If they don't seem to have something special, why not experiment with them? Tell them you are looking for something to do that won't let you be sad or unhappy, and maybe you can discover what it is together.

The bottom line is this: Being happy is often a choice. As Proverbs 3:18 says, "Wisdom is a tree of life to those who embrace her; happy are those who hold her tightly."

Be wise and choose happiness!

About the Authors

Greg and Patricia Mapes have been raising children for three decades, in conjunction with many years of business, ministry, revelatory, and pastoral experience.

An all-state athlete growing up in Michigan, Greg began his college education at the United States Air Force Academy. When his military career was shortened by a football injury, he attended the University of Michigan where he received a degree in engineering, followed by an MBA from Southern Methodist University. Presently he is the COO/CFO of Iformata Communications, a video network and video services provider.

Patricia grew up in St. Louis Park, Minnesota, and attended Gustavus Adolphus College and the University of Texas–Dallas. In 2006, she founded the Nexus Institute, a spiritual teaching and training group that includes Nexus Relief Organization and Nexus Connection. She is the author of *Reaching Your Destiny*, a training course that helps people overcome obstacles and be who they were created to be. It has been widely taught in the United States and Europe.

In addition to their business careers, Greg and Patricia have served in several churches, including Kansas City Christian Fellowship; Trinity Church in Fort Worth; and the Quad Cities Vineyard Christian Fellowship and New London Bridge, both of which Greg co-planted. For many years, Greg was the president of Streams Ministries International, and Patricia was chancellor of the Streams Institute for Spiritual Development. In addition to teaching, both of them have experience in prophetic and healing ministry.

They reside in North Sutton, New Hampshire, and have four adult children.

Bibliography and Suggested Resources

Sandford, John Loren and Paula. *Restoring the Christian Family.* Tulsa, OK: Victory House Publishers, 1979. (Reprinted by Charisma House, Lake Mary, FL: 2009.)

Sandford, John Loren. *Elijah Among Us.* Grand Rapids, MI: Chosen, 2002.

Lewis, C.S. *The Magician's Nephew.* London: The Bodley Head, 1955. (Reprinted by HarperCollins, New York: 2005.)

Loewi, O. *An Autobiographic Sketch, Perspectives in Biology and Medicine.* Vol IV, Iss I. Autumn 1960:17.

Kaempffert, Waldemar, ed. *A Popular History of American Invention.* Vol II. New York: Scribner's Sons, 1924. Page 385.

Schindler, George. "Dreaming of Victory," *New Scientist.* May 1997. Page 53.

Davis, Philip J. and Hersh, Reuben. *Descartes' Dream: The World According to Mathematics.* Orlando, FL: Harcourt Brace Jovanovich, Inc., 1986. (Reprinted by Dover Publications, Mineola, NY: 2005.)

Lord, Peter. *Hearing God.* Ada, MI: Baker Books, 1988.

Bibee, John. *The Spirit Flyer Series.* Westmont, IL: InterVarsity Press.

Conner, Kevin J. *Interpreting the Symbols & Types.* Portland, OR: City Christian Publishing, 1988.

Milligan, Ira. *Understanding the Dreams You Dream.* Shippensburg, PA: Treasure House, 1997.

www.fiveinarow.com

www.m-w.com

www.wordcentral.com

www.stirthewater.com

Spiritual Sensitivity Exercises

This section contains some simple exercises that you can do with your children to heighten their sensitivity to the Holy Spirit. These exercises teach children to pay attention to details and look for hidden depths in the revelations and dreams God gives them.

Seeing Colors: Part One
Objective: that children would learn to be more sensitive to the details God shows or speaks to them

1. Every day for a week, have your children pick a different color that they like or are interested in, such as red, blue, or yellow (not black, white, or gray).

2. Give them time (whatever seems age appropriate) to find and observe that color in their surroundings.

3. Do they see it:
   a. Inside?
   b. Outside?
   c. In manmade or fabricated objects?
   d. In nature?

4. How many different shades and tints of the color do they see?

5. How does the sheen of an object (shiny, dull, rough) affect the color?

6. Do they observe a difference between fabricated and natural instances of the color?

7. Can they distinguish between "new" color (such as a flower bud) and faded color (such as an older t-shirt)?

8. Do they think they have found "all" of that color? Nurture the idea that although they know what blue looks like and have found perhaps a hundred or more different shades of blue, there are still many more shades of blue that they haven't seen yet.

This exercise will also help your children differentiate between similar colors. For example, amber is a color that often appears in dreams or pictures, but if your children aren't familiar with amber, they may call the color yellow or orange. This limits their memory of the dream and could even potentially lend itself to errant interpretations.

Seeing Colors: Part Two
What you'll need: black, white, and gray paint chips (without color names listed on the front)

Day One
Objective: that children would learn to be more sensitive to the context of what God is showing them

1. Pick one of the paint chips and give your children time (whatever seems age appropriate) to find and observe that color in their surroundings.

2. Do they see it:
   a. Inside?
   b. Outside?
   c. In manmade or fabricated objects?
   d. In nature?

3. How many different shades and tints of the color do they see?

4. How does the sheen of an object (shiny, dull, rough) affect the color?

5. Do they observe a difference between fabricated and nat ural instances of the color?

6. If you chose black, eventually their observations will head toward gray. If white is the color, eventually they will start to select tans (white, off-white, cream, blush, etc.).

This is an important transition for children to comprehend, for revelatory people tend to be very "black and white" and not allow for "gray" areas. Here you can begin to add the concept of context and how it impacts observation. For example, if you were to paint the interior walls of your house some variation of cream or off-white, people may walk in and assume the walls were white. But if you were to paint the corresponding trim bright white, they would realize the walls were actually cream. Children need to learn that not everything is as it first appears.

Day Two
What you'll need: paint chips (black, white, or gray)

Objective: that children would learn to accept God's view of sit-uations and people and not have fixed or dogmatic worldviews

1. Chose one of the colors you didn't select previously and repeat steps 1 through 8 above.

2. When you are satisfied with your children's observation of black and white, take some time to discuss gray. Where is the line between black and gray? What about white and gray?

3. Lay out all the paint chips and see if the children can put them in order from white to gray to black.

4. Ask the children to then tell you where black ends and gray begins. If there are no descriptive labels on the paint chips, it may be difficult to tell, and different children may have different opinions. It won't be definitive.

We need to encourage our children to develop worldviews that aren't fixed or dogmatic. This will help them have more peace in their lives. If they believe that people and situations are only "good" or "bad," they will have a lot of unnecessary conflict, because their friends and leaders can't be perfect all the time. The earlier our children learn to be open to the entire picture, the more valuable their experiences will be.

For more interesting information about color, check out: www.colormatters.com/kids.

Exercise: The Timeline
What you'll need: a roll of paper about 12" wide and at least 20' long*

Objective: that children would be able to see how God has spoken to them over time

1. Use a large roll of paper to create a timeline of your chil
    dren's spiritual and personal history. They will have this for
    many years, so plan with them how it should be formatted.

2. Make a "0" at the upper left-hand corner of the timeline
    and then proceed forward. Let them draw pictures, write
    notes, etc. of their spiritual and significant life events. They
    should record all their dreams, words, visions, and experi
    ences with a point on the line and a title.

As children do this exercise, they will be able to put their life in perspective. They may begin to see that God speaks to them in certain ways at certain times of the year, that certain experiences helped them prepare for certain events, etc. It will be very revealing and inspiring for them to see how God has looked out for them all this time.

*Box suppliers such as ULINE carry paper that is 12" wide by over 90' long. That should be more than enough and costs about $25. Visit their site at www.uline.com.

Family Learning Activities

Museums
Children need to have their natural curiosity cultivated. Visiting museums will stimulate them; nurture inquisitiveness; and give them the context of time, history, and more. There is no substitute for the real thing, and so museums of all genres (art, science, history, natural history, "living history" farms and museums, engineering, etc.) should be regular destinations. Be sure to check out your local history as a family, too, because this will help your children learn to love and value the area they live in.

Sports
Sports are great venues in which children can learn leadership, courage, teamwork, and more. Look into the Boys and Girls Clubs, YMCA and YWCA, city-run recreation programs, etc.

Community activities
Activities such as community bands, plays, and other events are usually open to anyone. These not only connect children with people who could eventually become good friends, but they also can be wonderful learning and recreational activities that the whole family can enjoy.

Library
There is no substitute for a regular trip to the library. Let your children choose as many books as the library allows and then don't obligate them to read all of them. Let them explore, find out what interests them, and start to cultivate their own desires and tastes. This is not a performance activity; it is an exploration activity, and you want to leave a lot of room for the children's enthusiasms.

Book Clubs

Most children's book clubs will include both the mother and the children, which can be helpful. They may be age segregated (probably a good idea) or topic specific.

Spiritual Exercises

Stir the Water Prophetic and Seer Exercises are a good way for you and your family to learn and grow in how God speaks and gives us revelation. These exercises are designed to help you stop ignoring the spiritual activity around you and grow closer to God by practicing your spiritual giftings. Though the site is geared specifically for individuals, it can be used for families as well.

StirtheWater.com also includes an area where you can send in prophetic and seer questions and receive feedback. Go to www.stirthewater.com for more information.

Dream Interpretation

InterpretMyDream.com will help you understand God's mysterious metaphorical dream language. The site's dream interpreter training process is biblically based and includes Online Mentoring Groups, dream dictionary, Dream Chats, dreamer and interpreter forums, and dream journaling and submission. As with Stir the Water, the site is geared specifically for individuals, but it can be used for families as well. Go to www.interpretmydream.com for more information.

Booklists for Children and Families

Five in a Row Homeschool Curriculum
www.fiveinarow.com

Daniel 2:21 says, "'He gives wisdom to the wise and knowledge to the scholars.'" We should spend our lives gaining wisdom and understanding, which includes a healthy and perpetually expanding knowledge of God's creation around us.

Five in a Row provides fifty-five lesson plans that cover social studies, language, art, applied math, and science in a way that causes children to fall in love with learning.

Whether or not you are homeschooling your children, these are wonderful, entertaining, and educational books. Watch our web site, www.raisingspiritualchildrenbook.com, for information on book club plans and new resources.

Five in a Row (Ages 4–7)
Volume 1:

The Story About Ping by Marjorie Flack and Kurt Wiese
Lentil by Robert McCloskey
Madeline by Ludwig Bemelmans
A Pair of Red Clogs by Masako Matsuno
The Rag Coat by Lauren Mills
Who Owns the Sun? by Stacy Chbosky
Mike Mulligan and His Steam Shovel by Virginia Lee Burton
The Glorious Flight by Alice and Martin Provensen
How to Make an Apple Pie and See the World by Marjorie Priceman
Grandfather's Journey by Allen Say
Cranberry Thanksgiving by Wende and Harry Devlin

Another Celebrated Dancing Bear by Gladys Scheffrin-Falk
Papa Piccolo by Carol Talley
Very Last First Time by Jan Andrews
The Clown of God by Tomie DePaola
Storm in the Night by Mary Stoltz
Katy and the Big Snow by Virginia Lee Burton
Night of the Moonjellies by Mark Shasha
Stopping by Woods on a Snowy Evening by Robert Frost

Volume 2:

The Giraffe That Walked to Paris by Nancy Milton
Three Names by Patricia MacLachlan
Wee Gillis by Munro Leaf
Owl Moon by Jane Yolen
A New Coat for Anna by Harriet Ziefert
Mrs. Katz and Tush by Patricia Polacco
Mirette on the High Wire by Emily Arnold McCully
They Were Strong and Good by Alice and Robert Lawson
Babar, To Duet or Not to Duet based on characters by DeBrunhoff
The Story of Ferdinand by Munro Leaf
Down, Down the Mountain by Ellis Credle
Make Way for Ducklings by Robert McCloskey
The Tale of Peter Rabbit by Beatrix Potter
Mr. Gumpy's Motor Car by John Burningham
All Those Secrets of the World by Jane Yolen
Miss Rumphius by Barbara Cooney
The Little Red Lighthouse and the Great Gray Bridge by Hildegarde Swift
Follow the Drinking Gourd by Jeanette Winter
Harold and the Purple Crayon by Crockett Johnson
When I Was Young in the Mountains by Cynthia Rylant
Gramma's Walk by Anna Grossnickle Hines

Volume 3:

The Bee Tree by Patricia Polacco
Andy and the Circus by Ellis Credle
The Wild Horses of Sweetbriar by Natalie Kinsey-Warnock
Paul Revere's Ride by Henry Wadsworth Longfellow
Henry the Castaway by Mark Taylor
The Finest Horse in Town by Jacqueline Briggs Martin
Truman's Aunt Farm by Jama Kim Rattigan
The Duchess Bakes a Cake by Virginia Kahl
Andy and the Lion by James Daugherty
Daniel's Duck by Clyde Robert Bulla
Warm as Wool by Scott Russell Sanders
The Salamander Room by Anne Mazer
Climbing Kansas Mountains by George Shannon
Amber on the Mountain by Tony Johnston
Little Nino's Pizzeria by Karen Barbour

Volume 4:

Roxaboxen by Alice McLerran
The Raft by Jim LaMarche
Mailing May by Michael O. Tunnell
Snowflake Bentley by Jacqueline Briggs Martin
The Gullywasher by Joyce Rossi
Arabella by Wendy Orr
Higgins Bend Song and Dance by Jacqueline Briggs Martin
Cowboy Charlie by Jeanette Winter
Grass Sandals by Dawnine Spivak
Albert by Donna Jo Napoli
The Hickory Chair by Lisa Rose Fraustino
Hanna's Cold Winter by Trish Marx
The Hatmaker's Sign Retold by Candace Fleming
The Pumpkin Runner by Marsha Diane Arnold
Angelo by David Macaulay

Beyond Five in a Row (Ages 8–12)

The Boxcar Children by Gertrude Chandler Warner
Homer Price by Robert McCloskey
Thomas Edison by Sue Guthridge
Betsy Ross by Ann Weil
Sarah, Plain and Tall by Patricia MacLachlan
Skylark by Patricia MacLachlan
The Story of George Washington Carver by Eva Moore
Helen Keller by Margaret Davidson
The Cricket in Times Square by George Selden
The Saturdays by Elisabeth Enright
Neil Armstrong-Young Flyer by Montrew Dunham
Marie Curie and the Discovery of Radium by Ann E. Steinkefor

Above and Beyond Five in a Row (Ages 12+)
Hitty: Her First Hundred Years by Rachel Field

Five in a Row just recently published *small talk* (lower case intended), a set of diagnostic tests and complete early childhood curriculum for dealing with the diagnosis and treatment of speech and language delays. The author is pediatric speech pathologist Cari Ebert. For more information, visit www.fiveinarow.com.

Executive coaching
Helping you find your path

www.CoachMapes.com

CONNECTING TO GOD
CONNECT WITH OTHERS

Nexus Connection is a transformational teaching and equipping ministry focused on prophecy, dreams, and spiritual living.

We are dedicated to helping

people fulfill God's purpose for their

lives and experience deeper, fuller

relationships, both with God

and others.

Experience **Nexus Connection**:

How do you reach your destiny?

What's holding you back?

God drew us to Him decades ago in a powerful and supernatural manner. It is our intent to impart to others all that God has imparted to us.
— Patricia Mapes, founder

Do you feel like something is missing in your life?

How do you discover and conquer your shortcomings?

Visit **www.NexusConnection.org** for contact information, training tools, blog, online store, forum, and more.

Visit the companion website:

WWW.RAISINGSPIRITUALCHILDRENBOOK.COM

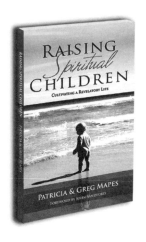

Raise up a child in the way he should go, and when he is old, he will not depart from it.
— Proverbs 22:6

CHECK THE WEBSITE REGULARLY FOR:

UPDATED FORUMS

VBS SUPPLEMENTS

PRACTICAL SELF-HELP TOOLS

ACTIVITIES FOR CHILDREN, PARENTS, GRANDPARENTS

AND MORE!

REACHING YOUR DESTINY

A NEXUSCONNECTION COURSE

What hidden issues are keeping
you from being all God wants you to be?

This two-and-a-half-day training course will walk you

through the biblical process of gaining victory

over *mental, emotional,* and *spiritual roadblocks.*

Open the door to a life of godly abundance!

Draw nearer to God and your destiny,

and discover *physical, emotional, creative,*

revelatory, and *financial* abundance in your life.

Nexus Connection: Prophecy, Dreams, and Spiritual Living

For more information, go to
www.NexusConnection.org.

Notes

Notes